EMBRACE IT
WHILE YOU
CHASE IT

SHAUN WORTHY

Copyright © 2018 Shaun Worthy

All rights reserved.

. No part of this publication may be reproduced in whole or in part, or stored in a retrieval system, or transmitted in any form or by any means, electronic, mechanical, photocopying, recording, or otherwise, without written permission of the publisher.N

All rights reserved.

ISBN -10: 1-7324677-7-3

ISBN-13: 978-1-7324677-7-4

DEDICATION

Thank you, GOD, for all my setbacks and failures, which transformed my pain into purpose.

I dedicate this book to my cousin Marcus Evans who passed away in 2014 as the result of a shooting in Oakland California, my auntie Juanita Evans who passed in 2015 and my auntie Rhonda Evans who recently passed away after 20+ years of dialysis. To my inspirations Pearlie Mae my mama, my son and young prince Javian Jerome, my sister Shantel, my niece Dominique and my two nephews Charles aka "Boogie" and Neff Christopher. To my other family and friends. To all the individuals who don't believe that they have a purpose and potential to be, do and have whatever they want as long as they work for it. To everyone who ever took the time to pour into me and gave me life to do the same for others. To everyone who doubted me, without you I would have never pushed so hard and took personal responsibility to create my own success. To all the young adults who struggle to thrive, know that you have what it takes to succeed you just have to activate it. To the young men who grew up without fathers to teach them the tools they needed to become a man, and the young ladies who didn't have a father to show them what "true love" looks like.

This book is also dedicated to the people who need another point of view in life and want to transform their struggles into strengths. Individuals who need to understand that passion and purpose are truly essential to success. It's dedicated to helping individuals who have been impacted by life in any way, develop their skills and create an identity for themselves. One of the best ways to learn is through someone else's experiences, so I willingly share mine in hopes that it will help you understand what's possible for you as well.

Embrace everything life offers!

CONTENTS

DEDICATION iii

AUTHOR'S PREFACE vii

01 // Embrace It While You Chase It 1

02 // Adapting the Growth Mindset 19

03 // Passion + Purpose= Paychecks 27

04 // Leadership Is Behavior, Not Position 47

05 // Skill Development 55

06 // The Lion & The Gazelle 83

07 // Principles Over Emotions 99

08 // Grind for a Reason, not a season 107

09 // Adversity Breeds Excellence 111

10 // The I 'AM WORTHY' Philosophy 117

11 // Why You Aren't Winning (BONUS CHAPTER) 121

ABOUT THE AUTHOR 133

AUTHOR'S PREFACE

This book is a unique blend of knowledge that I have acquired through street, formal and self-education. I believe that our experiences are one of our best teachers and that if we embrace these lessons being taught, we can tap into an unlimited amount of potential and power within ourselves. If we are to be successful, we cannot compare ourselves with others. Our biggest competition is with ourselves as we develop the discipline needed to become who we are meant to be. Success is not a "one size fits all," "only for certain people," or even "unreachable to the average person" type of result.

Take me for example; I managed to turn my misfortune into my biggest asset and transfer my skills from the streets into becoming an entrepreneur whose passion turned into paychecks. Now, instead of contributing to the problem, I've dedicated my life to creating solutions to the problem by helping youth and disadvantaged individuals break free of the stigmas, stereotypes and negative cycles they face.

It's our obligation to *use* the gifts we are given; we are being selfish when we don't. Sometimes those gifts are wrapped in adversity, pain, and struggle, but when we invest in fully unwrapping them, the real potential of those gifts is revealed.

Shaun Worthy

Get out and chase your dreams no matter how crazy it looks.

—Shanice Williams

01 EMBRACE IT WHILE YOU CHASE IT

Embrace It While You Chase It. This saying developed from an experience I had a couple of years before writing this book. I had a '98 Crown Vic that decided to break down about 2 miles from my house. I tried calling home for a ride, but it was late, so no one answered. With no other options, I grabbed my valuables out of the car and started walking home (with an attitude of course). As I trudged towards home, I began to think about how much I needed the car and this and that, when it hit me. I wasn't dead, life had just unexpectedly punched me in the face, and I had to accept that punch like I had every other one.

I logged onto Facebook Live to inspire others with my epiphany. I just started running my mouth about my situation and how I was remaining positive when I said it... "You just have to 'embrace it while you chase it.'" It fell out of my mouth like the last answer to the million-dollar question on "Who Wants to Be a Millionaire." When hash tags with the saying began popping up in the comments, I knew I had something. It's during unforeseeable moments like this that greatness often happens.

So, what exactly is the concept of "Embrace It While You Chase It?" Simply put, it's a mentality that has no limits or excuses. When life punches you in the face, do you fight back? Are you willing to do what is required to live the life you want? Adversity is something every human comes up against, but within it lies excellent opportunity. If you can look at a challenge as a process and choose to work through it, you will build a muscle of resilience. This resilience will prepare you to lift, push and overcome any adversity, in ways you could never have imagined.

Many things will happen in your life that causes discomfort, pain, and uncertainty. The key to overcoming those obstacles is to run towards them instead of away from them. I know, I know... you're probably thinking "Why would I do that?" Well, the answer is simple. The best way to handle a challenge is to face the problem head-on. Most individuals fall into the trap of running from, or avoiding challenges that occur in their lives; don't fall into this trap. You may not always be able to put out the fires or even partially resolve the issues, but you do build a mindset that enables you to embrace difficult situations. To illustrate this point, allow me to tell you my story.

Growing up, I lived the "embrace it while you chase it" mentality to the fullest. The problem was, I didn't apply the concept to the right things. At 12 years old I started smoking weed, by 14 I was selling it, and by 15 I could get my hands on anything and everything. Not good. Why? Because one choice that I made at the age of 12, that seemed so insignificant and so harmless at the time, led me to make many other decisions that could have ruined, and almost did ruin my life. Cocaine and ecstasy became not only my drugs of choice to sell but also my drugs of choice to use. Before I knew it, I was lost in the rat race I was trying to avoid. Eventually, one thing led to another, and four months after turning 18, I was arrested on five charges and facing ten years in prison. Keep in mind that before all of this happening, I had already been to juvenile detention five times for petty crimes, including residential burglary, organized crime, and drug distribution.

Remember, I told you that I've always embraced adversity while chasing whatever I was after, so when the time came to serve my sentence, I did three out of the five years "on the chin;" meaning I took ownership for my actions. I didn't expect or ask anyone to shorten my sentence or take a plea deal from the prosecutor. I stood trial facing ten years in prison, and was sentenced to five.

See, during this part of my life, I embraced adversity by giving in to the false idea that the only way I could survive it, was by becoming a part of it. This idea, in turn, caused me to chase what I "thought" being a part of it had to offer me: a euphoric high that rid me of my worries, and fast money that gave me a sense of security; both of which were temporary.

Now here is where the story gets good.

When I was finally released from prison, I was 21 years old with a 2-year-old son. I had never talked to my father or even knew what he looked like for that matter, so I didn't know too much about how to be a father myself. I did know, however, that I needed to be and wanted to be the best father I could to my son. Little did I know the opportunity was about to present itself in a significant way...but not without adversity. This time, however, I was going to embrace that adversity the right way. I wasn't going to give into it, I was going to fight it...and more importantly, I was going to beat it. Furthermore, I was going to chase after the right thing, for the right reason. I needed to obtain custody of my son, but I needed a good lawyer and didn't have the kind of money it was going to take to hire one, so...I appointed myself. I had studied some law while I was incarcerated, so I took that knowledge and added some more to it to be prepared to represent myself in court. It worked. Three years after my release from prison, I was awarded full custody of my son.

Today, not much has changed. Well, except the fact that I'm now the author of a book, a legal and successful business owner and I work with youth in my community to empower, educate, and mentor them to be successful. See what I did? I took that same mentality that landed me in prison and used it to land me my son and my purpose. Can you say "Embrace It While You Chase It?"

This mentality changed my life when I started embracing everything life threw at me; the pain and difficulty, the small wins, my purpose, etc. It became easier to navigate through life because I realized most things that happen in our lives occur because of our own decision making, rather than random adversity. I believe in cause and effect. The small things over time build up, so if you avoid them, eventually you will have a bunch of beasts that you fed and ignored; that is, until you ran out of food, they got loose and turned on you.

It's essential that you embrace the unknown, uncomfortable, uninvited circumstances you face. You can't control everything that happens, but you can control the choices you make about the things that happen, and you must understand that every single decision you make will have a result. If you give as much effort as possible to do what is in your control, then you can create opportunities for the things you cannot. The key is to focus on aligning your decisions with intent and purpose. It makes the ride less bumpy and the experience more enjoyable. You can't pick, plan, or force anything to happen the way you want it to, so instead of focusing on what you can't control, you need to focus on what you can, and prepare yourself for the possible results, be them good or bad. You stunt your growth when you avoid the process of life; don't avoid it, prepare for it.

Once you adopt this mentality, you will become more in tune with what I'm saying, as it is more of a feeling than a thought. At first, yes, you will need to train your mind to think this way, but sooner than later you will embody it. It will become second nature to you because your intent and purpose will be attached to your actions. Your mindset about adversity will begin to shift and grow, and you will soon realize that the fastest way to growth is through it. No longer will you avoid the thing that will help you unlock your potential.

MAKING LIFE'S CHALLENGES OUR GREATEST OPPORTUNITIES

Section #1 Adversity

Embracing Challenge While Overcoming Adversity!

I turned everything negative in my life into a positive, and I had this particular mentality that enabled me to do so. Life is going to test you with your own set of unique challenges and circumstances, so don't make the mistake of looking at what others are going through and trying to compare it to your situation. A wise man once told me, "What you go through is important, but not as much as what you do with what you go through." We all have to endure struggles, and we all have to make decisions regarding those struggles. Sometimes these are tough choices, but you can't allow yourself to be so consumed with what you're going through, that you become paralyzed and are unable to create a plan for how you're going to take action and solve the problem.

I have had my share of adversity and struggle, but who hasn't? What I know now is that when I was young, I put myself through a lot of abuse, drugs and other dysfunction that wasn't necessary. As a hustler, addict and miseducated young black man, I became a victim of the streets. I remember being told that I was looking at a ten-year prison sentence. I didn't flinch when the judge said it for one reason and one reason only; I knew my choices had signed me up for it. I have always dealt with my problems that way. If I choose to do something regardless of what happens, then I have to take ownership of it on the chin. There have been plenty of times when adversity consumed my life, but it never stopped me from continuing to embrace who I would become. I knew I wasn't going through all of that adversity for no reason, but I wasn't willing to make the same choices and do the same things expecting a different result. I had to turn that struggle into strength and not allow my past to determine my destiny.

Success in life depends on being strong individuals with clear goals and an unbeatable spirit. Guess what? I have good news, and I have bad news. The bad news is, unfortunately, most of us aren't born that way. The good news is, we have the power to take our life experiences and use them to help us grow into that individual. Growth can occur when you enter willingly into situations that will cause you to grow, or from how you choose to react to circumstances that present themselves without your prior approval. Most of us spend our lives trying to avoid adversity when we should be learning how to accept the fact that it exists but can be overcome. Now I'm not saying go looking for it; I'm saying that when it presents itself (and it inevitably will), you should embrace it as an opportunity to become a better person through your interaction with it. Every time you encounter adversity, it creates an opportunity for you to grow both personally and professionally, and it develops integrity in your character that you can't obtain anywhere else.

Hardships often prepare ordinary people for an extraordinary destiny. Embracing your challenges is nothing more than accepting, taking control, and including them as part of your journey. In the midst of life's difficulties, we tend to fight against adversity until we get hit with more during the process. Then we often look for someone or something else to blame and become angry at whoever or whatever we decide is responsible for our discomfort. The problem with this is when we try to shift responsibility from ourselves to others, one it doesn't work and two we take away our power to solve the problem; that power we have is called integrity, and in this case, the power of integrity has to do with taking ownership of the situation.

Sometimes you cannot control your environment, so you must work to change your attitude and see things from a different perspective. By tapping into your potential, you will learn skillful ways to deal with your struggles and avoid the habit of defeating yourself mentally. Every time you embrace a challenge or obstacle, you become more intelligent and brave, and it takes a collection of those experiences to develop and grow in life. If you train your mind to be more understanding, you'll uncover that the real source of your unhappiness was the failure to educate, manage, and transform your mental state.

Show me someone who has done something worthwhile, and I'll show you someone who has overcome adversity.

~ Lou Holtz

Section #2 The Gift

The meaning of life is to find your gift.
The purpose of life is to give it away.

~ Pablo Picasso

First and foremost, if you are reading this book, you have a gift. No, it's not reading. Lol. Every person is born with a gift that they naturally possess, called a talent. Each human was put in this world with the ability to do something well. We cheat ourselves and the world if we don't use it to the best of our ability. Having talent, however, is only so useful without practice. Practice is a consistent work ethic that eventually produces skill. You ever heard the saying, "Hard work beats talent when talent doesn't work hard?" Without training your gift over time, you will never maximize its potential. Think of your talent as a knife blade that cuts well through certain things, but that if sharper, could cut through anything. Through repetition of practice, you are sharpening your talent to be a unique skill.

No matter your path, and regardless of your upbringing, you have authentic traits within your personality, talents, and ways of communicating and being motivated, that are different from those around you. Using what makes you different with purpose and developing it into something of value to others is the ultimate gift to yourself. Your gift isn't indeed a gift unless you share it with others. When you operate using your gift, you perform better, feel better, have more success, feel more fulfilled and get outstanding results. This concept is critical to understand. Most individuals never build, use or share their gifts with the world. If they do, it's small compared to what is possible. When you are authentic and gifted, it goes a long way.

What if I told you that success and satisfaction are within your reach and that all you need to do is discover it and purposefully and intentionally use your natural way of life, which I call your "unique talent or gift," every day? The ultimate goal in life is to align your career or business with your life and unique talent. When you figure out how to turn your passion into purpose, life will be more comfortable and more rewarding. That's what chapter 3 is all about.

The part that's difficult is making that happen. It takes time, experience, and drive. It's easy not to put that much effort into such a laborious process, but so many individuals will do things that are not their gift, and that they do not enjoy, using that same effort if not more! You have a choice; how bad do you want it?

My mentor always told me that most people want what it looks like, but not what it feels like, because once they feel it, they give up. If it were easy to use your gift everyone would be doing it, but that doesn't mean it's not possible for you, no matter your circumstances. Diamonds are created through extreme pressure and heat, and that is what it will take to develop your gift.

Three aspects of who you are come together to form your "unique talent," and create the foundation for how you bring value to the world. By exploring and understanding these three aspects of who you are, you can then purposefully and intentionally use them to drive your success:

Your Strengths

Capabilities that can be improved with practice, but that come naturally and can be developed into a unique skill.

Your Learning Styles

Ways you process and communicate information.

Your Motivation Styles

Ways you are motivated or compelled to action.

Discovering Your Gifts

I believe this is the most natural part of the process, but that it can be difficult if you haven't had experiences in life to help show you what your gifts may be. As you grow up, you notice that some things are more natural for you than others, such as playing sports, singing, dancing, problem-solving, etc. You recognize that, even without any practice, you seem to have an advantage. You're on to something. You're tapping into your gifts. Sometimes you might also have to get a couple of jobs, volunteer, or be willing to try new things to discover your gifts. Either way, every individual has an advantage over the next due to their unique talents. That's not by accident, that's a gift given explicitly to you. Once it's discovered, the next step is to use it.

I discovered my gift when I spoke to the leadership class at Stahl Jr. High. My whole life I've loved to talk. The gift of gab is just something I'm blessed with having. The problem was that up until then I had only used it to get into trouble most of the time because I honestly didn't know the gift it was or the power it could have until I had a story to tell.

I had been using my Facebook platform to create motivational messages but had no experience speaking in front of people. The only thing that made me comfortable doing it was that my favorite teacher Mr. Marcoe invited me, and he was excited for his current students to hear a success story from one of his past students.

First off, I didn't think I was successful; but I did want to share my story with students from my old school, so I went and spoke. After it was over, I thought I did horrible, but because I poured my heart out with passion, they loved it! I still have all of the testimonies they wrote me. I'm going to keep it one hundred; I straight up cried when I realized that my story could touch people.

Things I had been doing well my whole life, speaking and living, were the gifts that helped me add value to other people's lives. It was, and still is a challenge developing and learning how to turn my talent into a skill, but I haven't looked back since and my life has not been the same. Every day I appreciate the opportunity to use my gift, and not selfishly, but with intent and purpose.

Using Your Unique Gift

The key to creating success and fulfillment is to align your gift with your purpose and intent. "What does that mean?" you might ask. Aligning your gift with your purpose and intent means using your talents and skills to provide real value to the unique thing you were created to accomplish in life.

For your career, it means purposely using your gift to provide the best possible value to your employer and to improve your productivity. As an employee, you are valued and compensated for what you bring to the table. Imagine if you came to work each day providing real value and knocking all tasks out of the park!

In your business, you want to provide products and services that are aligned with your gift. It's hard to give the best service possible or stand behind your product if it's not aligned with your talents. Doing this creates a value for your clients and customers that makes them want to return and do business with you regardless of competition because your ability is unique.

In your life, purposely use that gift or talent to create and enhance your relationships, and be of the highest value to your family and friends. When you can see the impact you have on people's lives, it makes life more meaningful and gives you a more significant purpose for your gift. You have a responsibility in life to make the world better with your gifts and talents. It's one of the most unselfish decisions you can make, and it will benefit you in ways you won't understand until you experience it. Developing your sense of where you want your life to go is difficult for most. It's a foreign place, and you don't speak the language. Here are four ways you can begin to understand your true self, and in turn help yourself create the life you want on your terms.

Create Awareness

Creating awareness is key to understanding what will work for you and what won't. If you are aware of your strengths and weaknesses, then you can focus on what needs to improve and change. You will be able to find opportunities and resources that allow you to navigate with purpose.

Create Vision

Creating a clear vision of where you want to will require self-awareness of your strengths and values. It helps you navigate through difficult times and gives you a picture to place your goals into. Having vision is a long-term thinking process that is created by you.

Create Goals

There are different ways to set goals and the way you approach your goals will depend on your unique vision. Your goals may require small, abstract steps, more massive, more concrete actionable steps, or a combination of both, such as with a financial goal or the goal of starting a business. Setting dates for completion of your goals is also very important, as it helps to hold you accountable to your dreams.

Take Action

Taking action is the most challenging step. When you create awareness, vision, and goals, you are deciding to make a change. The process of taking action requires effort, consistency, and uncomfortable situations. Taking action is the step that shows you how badly you want to accomplish your goals. Planning is easy, but most never complete the most crucial part...executing that plan.

Section #3 The Journey

Life is a continuous process of growth. Without being stretched you won't know what your true capabilities are. It's on you to maximize this opportunity by using your talents to impact the ones you love and the rest of the world.

All the people in this world take a journey called life. It is full of ups and downs, joy, pain and many other gains and losses. Your journey will be filled with lessons, adversities, pleasures, celebrations and special memories that will ultimately lead you to your purpose in life.

Some of these challenges you encounter will test your courage, strengths, weaknesses, and faith. Along the way, you will come to obstacles that stand between the paths that you are intended to take and the paths that you are not. To follow the correct path, you must overcome these problems. Sometimes these obstacles are blessings in a costume, and you don't realize it at the time. How you react to what you face will determine what kind of outcome the rest of your journey will have.

"My mission in life is not merely to survive, but to thrive; and to do so with some passion, some compassion, some humor, and some style."

Maya Angelou

Here are 5 Ways to Develop the "Embrace It While You Chase It" Mentality:

Learn About Yourself

The most important knowledge is self-knowledge. When you begin to learn about yourself, you can navigate through life with purpose and potential that continues to grow.

Fail Forward

Nobody likes to fail. It's a typical mindset to accept failure, but the ability to quickly put it in the rearview and embrace the teachings of failure will be life-changing. Since I have never met an individual who hasn't experienced some failure, I think it's about what you do after. Do you give up or keep going?

Turn Temporary Losses Into Lifetime Lessons

You learn more from losing than winning. Each life experience has a lesson attached, good or bad. You must focus even harder during the bad times, to get the important lessons from them that will prepare you for the next level of life.

Live With Passion

Attach your passion to what you want to do in life, then design a plan to pursue it. I'd rather be challenged by chasing my dreams than to be successful in trying to avoid them.

Become Driven

Motivation, like cologne or perfume, doesn't last long. When it begins to wear off, you will need the drive and discipline to keep going. Motivation requires having a purpose for what you are doing. When you take the pain in your life and apply it to accomplish your goals that create drive. When you have the drive, you will do anything necessary to achieve what you set out to do.

> *Once your mindset changes, everything on the outside changes along with it.*
>
> *—Steve Maraboli.*

02 ADAPTING THE GROWTH MINDSET

I had trouble becoming the individual I needed to be to achieve my success because I didn't believe in the one thing that I could control...myself. I allowed everything to limit me; T.V., my teachers, my mom and the label society wanted to place on me. I'm not lying when I say that I had zero self-confidence and self-worth. It was hard to see anything coming out of my future that was positive. My whole life I had been overcoming challenges, but I didn't understand the power I held inside myself or how to use it to my benefit at the time. I just knew I was willing to face obstacles and find ways to move past them. Little did I know, I already possessed part of the mindset I needed to help turn me into the man I am today.

The process of embracing this mindset began in prison. OG's and old heads would speak life into me by giving me advice and game, on how to live a better life without making decisions that hurt myself, my family, my community, and so much more. I started thinking about what I would do when I got out. My mind grew, and I began to feed it things that related to my interests. I like personal development; learning how to become a better person. Ironically, I was never in many environments where this was talked about until I was in prison. The part that interested me the most was how I was able to relate to the books I read, even though most of them were written from a different perspective. The authors would discuss how the topics they had written about applied to their own lives, which in turn helped me see how I could use those topics in my life. I soon learned a lot about myself and life in general.

It wasn't easy at first. One major struggle I had was my inability to read well. I had never read a book from beginning to end or even thought about doing it. Even if it was interesting enough to keep my attention, I still struggled with reading the whole book. The first one I was able to do so with was "Million Dollar Habits" by Brian Tracy. It taught me that a lot of the game I had learned in the streets was universal and that my skills were transferable. That meant I could still use the skills and information I had learned, but apply them to the world in a different, positive way.

Coming to this realization was when real growth started happening, and my confidence started building. I was challenged during this growth process the most, and truly adopted the growth mindset into my life when I fought for custody of my son. The amount of adversity I dealt with as an uneducated young black man, didn't have a chance against the heart, passion, and tenacity I had after getting out of prison. I channeled all the positive processes I speak about in this book towards gaining custody of my son. All of the reading, discipline, resilience and the "Embrace It While You Chase It" mentality paid off.

Without growth in my life, I would have returned to selling drugs or other criminal activities. Instead, I decided to apply the same potential that I had towards negative things in the past, to positive things in the present and the future. I wasn't built for the typical 9-5 lifestyle, but that didn't mean I had to channel that into negativity. So I didn't. I challenged myself like the streets did by developing the skills I already had to become a professional by my design.

Life will not help you reach your potential; you must grow into it. Your mind is a force of unlimited power. How you use it can either create or destroy you. Not believing in yourself can prevent you from reaching your full potential, while believing in yourself can push you toward becoming the person you've only ever imagined. Belief and focus play a massive role in your mindset.

Key Ingredients to Growth:

Effort

Challenges

Mistakes

Feedback

Now, this chapter is inspired by an audiobook I listened to called "Mindset, The New Psychology of Success" by Carol Dweck,

Ph.D. The book is a must-read for anyone who enjoys this chapter. I want you to understand the importance of learning to develop a growth mindset, which will help you reach success in all areas of your life: career, school, business, relationships, etc. I want to share with you my experiences with and perspectives on the "Growth" and "Fixed" mindsets.

The Fixed Mindset

People who have a fixed mindset believe their natural abilities, such as their intelligence or talent, is going to be enough to get them to and keep them where they want to be; that talent alone creates success—without effort. A "fixed mindset," according to my research, believes that to carry on the wisdom of being smart or skilled, you must strive for success and avoid failure at all costs. These are all incorrect and harmful ways of thinking. Our personality, drive, and even our setbacks grow out of our mindset. In a fixed mindset, when the aim is to get recognition, the person continually tries to prove them self and is extremely sensitive to being wrong or making a mistake. Failure brings them doubt, degrades their character, and destroys their confidence. As a result, a person with a fixed-mindset always feels worried and is vulnerable to setbacks or criticisms.

When I was young, I had a lot of issues with growing out of my shell. I had a hard time finding a way to build confidence, develop skills, and be exposed to people who had growth mindsets. A lot of what I heard was people doubting themselves, and having unrealistic views of success. Eventually, I adopted the same mentality. I went into the streets thinking I had to and that I wasn't supposed to live a better life. If I were doing something positive, I would give up as soon as the challenge or difficulty arose; it didn't matter if it was football, school, or just life in general. I was immersed in living up to the limits others had placed on me, and even worse, I used those limits against myself without even knowing my capabilities. My mindset was fixed into becoming comfortable like everyone around me.

Almost no one in my family has ever owned a successful business, attended college, or done anything that caused them to develop out of their comfort zones. This lack of development is not their fault nor mine. It's a vicious cycle that has been created by complacency and a fixed mindset. Not everything I did was affected by it immediately, but over time I would start to break my willpower. The only way I would begin to think and move differently was if my environment, conversations and what I allowed myself to believe changed. I started to like the feeling of defeating challenges and overcoming obstacles, and before I knew it, I was feeding off of those feelings.

Instead of avoiding discomfort, I embraced it with the same courage I had faced any other uncomfortable situation. The difference now was that I controlled what I could and didn't let anything outside of that affect me. I changed my circle from people who thought within a fixed mindset, to people who operated from within a growth mindset. In no way was it easy to make those changes either; I'm talking about family, friends and everything I knew and was comfortable with had to go if they or it weren't aligning with my new found way of thinking.

Many of us think that our behavior and skills are permanently set during early childhood and by the environment where we grew up. If you think this way, then it means you believe that you possess only a specific amount of intelligence, a particular personality, a distinct moral character, and that you can't develop those qualities through consistent efforts of improvement. These beliefs aren't right; there are thousands of success stories about individuals taking what they are given and maximizing it. Likewise, if you choose to believe that your qualities and circumstances are not merely something you've been given and forced to live with, you will cultivate them through your efforts to reach your full potential just like the thousands of stories before you.

Growth Mindset

People who have a growth mindset believe that their most natural abilities can be developed through commitment and hard work. Intellect and talent are just the starting point. This view creates a love of learning and a resilience that is important for achieving greatness. Almost all the individuals considered greats have had these qualities. Learning how to use this mindset creates an advantage and separates you from others in the worlds of business, education, sports, etc. It also enhances your relationships. The growth mindset is also about achieving mastery and expertise, so people who have it view failure as a form of feedback about their performance, not as a form of judgment about their personality, potential or value. They're not sensitive to constructive criticisms, and setbacks don't hurt them in the same ways as in a fixed mindset. The growth mindset seeks a challenge and believes that failure is not a result of unintelligence but an opportunity to experience growth and development. The mindset you choose to embrace plays a significant role in how you live your life, determining whether or not you become who you want to be and whether or not you achieve your goals.

Below are a few examples of brilliant, growth-minded individuals who mastered music, literature, science, sports, and business. A growth mindset allowed them to achieve the incredible things that make them well known. Most importantly, however, they are proof that we can change our mindset to achieve success and fulfillment at any stage of our lives.

- Michael Jordan
- Warren Buffett
- Martin Luther King Jr
- Jackie Robinson
- Tom Brady
- Mark Cuban
- Malcolm X
- Rosa Parks
- Ellen DeGeneres
- Harriet Tubman
- Eric Thomas
- Thomas Edison
- Barack Obama
- Helen Keller
- Katherine Johnson

> *When you catch a glimpse of your potential, that is when passion is born.*
>
> —Zigziglar.

03 PASSION + PURPOSE = PAYCHECKS

I remember when I got out of prison. I had $100, a bus ticket and no idea what I was going to do with my life. I knew I didn't want to work for someone else, but I had to provide for my son positively and stay out of trouble. I took any job I could get: taking inventory, working in warehouses, construction, etc. I had 6-8 jobs in the first few years of my release. Honestly, I was looking for an opportunity that would change my circumstances so that I wouldn't ever have to answer to #329032 again.

One year after being released, a friend called me about an opportunity to make a lot of money through a home business in the "Network Marketing" industry. The company provided people with services that they used in their houses on a daily basis. This opportunity interested me. Not because of the potential income, however. One thing I wasn't focused on as much as most people were, was the money; more than that, I wanted ownership, purpose and to be an entrepreneur. I sold drugs from ages 12-18, and even though I wasn't blind to the potential money that could be made from doing it, money wasn't my primary interest. I learned a lot about myself while in prison; one of those things being that I loved entrepreneurship.

Most of the skills I had learned from hustling could be applied positively in my life if I became an entrepreneur and owned businesses. I realized I could make a living doing something similar to street hustling (but legit), and also help others with no boss or clock in time; this meant I could do it before, during or after work. I didn't know what to do to become an entrepreneur then, but I knew that I was going to be one. I was still working dead-end jobs doing general labor that I hated, so I took the first opportunity, risk or whatever you want to call it, that was presented to me. I invested my paycheck into my first business endeavor. It failed. I learned invaluable lessons, however, and experienced a taste of the lifestyle I wanted.

Now I didn't make money in the first three businesses I attempted to establish, but it helped me to start developing that growth mindset I talked about in chapter two, and it also helped me gain experience. I failed but I failed forward, and when I learned the lesson, I applied it to my next opportunity. That's why I believe that in life you don't take a loss, you learn a lesson. I went from selling other people's products, to marketing Shaun Worthy's products and services! Oh, there were plenty of times I didn't think I was capable! I let other people's opinions become my own, found excuses for not putting in my full effort and to avoid taking action, and even expected what I wanted to be handed to me, which were all characteristics of a fixed mindset. It was changing my mindset and deciding that I wasn't going to look for shortcuts, expect success to come overnight or go back to selling drugs that helped me grow from those experiences and increase my resilience.

Years ago I was talking to a lady, trying to make a sale for my business. I spoke way too long about things that had nothing to do with the product, but when I was done she said, "I'm extremely motivated; can you call me Monday morning for some motivation?" Now, I had talked my way into and out of a thing or two in my day, but I hadn't imagined I would talk my way into a situation like that... especially without an answer! I knew it was a sign, but I didn't know what it meant.

I am grateful that my journey brought me to such a significant moment in my life. That sign led to the discovery of my real passion. I no longer talked just to be talking. Nope, now I had a reason, and that reason was to motivate people. My passion was motivational speaking.

This chapter was written to help you connect what it is you are passionate about to your purpose. Once you can combine both with experience, it will become a paycheck! I am a living example that this is possible. I initially had a difficult time finding my purpose in life. I am a passionate person, and as a result of this, I discovered that I was excited about several things, but it wasn't until I started volunteering around youth and had an opportunity to speak, that I understood how to transform my passions into a career. Once I did, however, it changed my life forever.

Now I speak in jr. high and high schools in my area, I've created the clothing brand "Worthy Hustle Apparel," and I'm Founder and CEO of I AM WORTHY Youth Development, a youth development company that is now contracted with multiple school districts and a juvenile justice system. I guess you could say I found it; "it" being my purpose. I have only just opened the door to my purpose, however. I haven't even begun seeing all I'm truly capable of or where my purpose will take me.

My inspiration for writing this chapter stems from my desire to help you avoid the difficulties I had to endure, by helping you understand that there is a formula for real success and this is it! Success is not about material things. The actual measure of success is fulfillment, and guess what living out your passion does for you? It makes you fulfilled! Acting on your passion can do so much more too if you activate the formula!

First and foremost, there is no secret method to finding your passion. That is what stumps most people. People often ask me, "How do I find my passion?" I always respond by providing methods I've used and have seen work. For example, volunteering, serving, anything that doesn't involve just a wage or paycheck, is one strategy for discovering your purpose. Now I'm not saying you can't find your passion while working or making money, but I know that if you enjoy doing it for free or without a reward, you have a love for it. Another way to find your passion is by observing the things you give more of your energy to freely. Passion is more than just enthusiasm or excitement; passion is ambition materialized into actions fueled by as much of our heart, mind, body, and soul as possible for us to give.

As I indicated before, your passion is something that you could do every single day and not get paid for it. For example, some artists start off making art based on passion. Money does not drive their interest in creating art; passion drives it. As a result, some artists realize that their passion is their purpose, and they take it to the next level which results in the paycheck.

A paycheck in this chapter doesn't refer to just money. Some people have a passion for serving and helping people, but they don't worry about money; they're more interested in the joy that comes from making an impact or providing an excellent experience for people in need. The reward of impacting people, places, or things is a paycheck in itself, creating movements, businesses, and brands based on passions. It's all about being purposeful with your passion and having a specific intent on using it to benefit the world.

Section 2
IKIGAI

You have to have an ikigai. When I first saw this word I thought it wasn't spelled right. Then I started researching and watching videos, and in my research, I discovered that this is the most critical thing to our human existence! Without it, we go through life in a meaningless or unfulfilling way. The word comes from a Japanese island called Okinawa, said to be home to the largest population of centenarians in the world. Now, you may be asking "What is a centenarian?" Centenarians are people who are one hundred or more years old. I'm also guessing you might be wondering why they live so long; is it something in the water? Do they have better genes? Is it what they eat? Well, not exactly. You see, even though all of those things could be true, the reason for their long lives that we're going to discuss in this book, is that the Japanese believe in having an ikigai or reason for living.

One of the many mistakes I've made in my life was believing that money led to fulfillment. I loved to make money; I loved it so much I made a lot of bad choices and hurt a lot of people trying to obtain it. I'm not saying that money isn't essential, I just made it my number one concern, and I didn't realize what that was doing to me. We all know that money is a necessity. It's up there right along with oxygen, food, water, and shelter. In most cases, you need money to access food and water, and the way things are going now, it seems like soon we might have to start paying for oxygen too.

What happened to me was I became apart of a rat race, just a different kind than the typical 9-5 lifestyle. My race was in the streets. When it came to money I could never make enough, I could never spend enough, and I always had to chase something to sustain my grind. When I got locked up I started thinking about how unhappy my life was, how pursuing my next bag (a come up or money) didn't fulfill me. By the time I realized that the real cost of doing what I was doing was far too high and not worth the consequences that came with it, I was already being called "329032." The parts of the lifestyle I was living that I considered "good" didn't last very long and did more harm than good in the end. You can ask anyone; Sean "Diddy" Combs was right when he said "more money, more problems."

Even if you're not in the streets chasing money, you can still be chasing the wrong things and have no real reason for being alive. Most of the STUFF we look at as valuable is material in nature. If obtaining material things is the only reason why you live, then I doubt you've made it this far in the book to read this, let alone are very happy in life period. The insatiable desire to only obtain material things shortens the lifespan of the materialistic person's mindset towards the value of what they already have or what's important. I spoke earlier in this chapter about my formula: passion + purpose = paychecks, which I think is simple but has a deeper meaning when it comes to the paychecks part. When you do something for a more profound sense than to obtain money, it unlocks a door that few even know exist. The door to fulfillment.

Living is infectious. It's like having a virus you don't ever want to cure. I don't think it's contagious though until you align the reason for being alive with your life. For many people, striving to find their purpose in life can relate to a rollercoaster ride, filled with many twists, turns and flips. Some blindly follow passions that aren't based in reality, then wind up feeling discouraged when their dreams don't materialize. Others find themselves in a career that brings them money and status but isn't fulfilling. In both cases, over time, their sense of purpose can begin to fade. Your ikigai has a few qualities that separate it from the "follow your passion for your purpose" cliche phrases we hear all the time:

It's challenging.

Your ikigai should lead to mastery and growth.

It's your choice.

You feel a certain degree of self-determination and freedom pursuing your ikigai.

It involves a commitment of time and belief, perhaps to a particular cause, skill, trade or group of people.

It boosts your well-being. Ikigai is associated with positive relationships and good health. It gives you more energy than it takes away.

The four key components that make up your ikigai are:

What you love (your passion)

What the world needs (your mission)

What you are good at (your vocation)

What you can get paid for (your profession)

As we go deeper into the chapter, we will talk about how these four components intersect and connect your passion to your purpose. You'll see a diagram that will explain how these components make up the formula: Passion + Purpose = Paychecks.

Most individuals who find their passion don't mind using it to make money, and there's nothing wrong with that. It's not a bad thing to make money from passion and purpose. It's something that I think everyone should attempt at some point in life. Understand, however, that making money is not the only intention of everyone who connects their passion to their purpose. Although not motivated by money, some people do things they are passionate about for money to both earn a living and still have fulfillment and purpose in their day to day lives. There are a lot of different ways to look at how passion drives you and how it can be connected to your purpose or something more significant.

The interesting part about the above examples is that though somewhat different, they are both the same in that their drive is their passion and their purpose. Most people find their passion on the way to their purpose, and so by default they inspire, educate, help and motivate others. Someone whose passion is to fulfill other's needs gets their reward by serving a purpose bigger than their own. An individual who uses their passion for solving a problem and creating an income is no different, and also has an impact on individuals, just not in the same way.

What I need you to understand the most is that when you follow your passion, sometimes it's about money and sometimes it's not. True, it is another way to create an income, but if that's your only focus, then you should probably consider staying at or getting yourself a 9-5. You will have to do a lot of free work along the way to creating income and opportunities from your passion; many people are passionate about something but don't understand there will be sacrifices and ups and downs. It is critical that the path you take is one you can walk without a reward or paycheck consistently motivating you.

A lot of people put in a lot of time, effort and sacrifices to see that paycheck. By the time the checks come, you will have put in a lot of work preparing and practicing. Most of the time you won't be paid (in the beginning), but you still have to be passionate about it. Don't get me wrong you can earn while you learn, which is making money in the process of developing yourself, but delayed gratification pays better and lasts longer. Take athletes for example. They put in years of practice in the backyard, in little leagues, on courts and the track, etc., before they even begin making money off their athletic ability; some never make any money. When you start out, you must invest the following without an immediate return on your investment:

Time

Money

Effort

Yourself

The world has changed with technology, culture, and values. It has created a wave of opportunity for people that live their dreams through their passions. If you understand social media or have an account, you have seen this first hand.

People use platforms like YouTube to share videos on their topic of interest. In return, they build a community of individuals with a mutual interest and passion that eventually transforms into endless opportunities. These opportunities come in the form of endorsements, free products, and services; even T.V. opportunities, and that's not even half of the benefits they could receive.

I want to tell you that it's NOT as easy as it sounds, but it's possible. There are a couple of things you MUST know before thinking you can make money. I'm going to giving you 3 of the most important principles behind the Passion + Purpose = Paychecks formula:

Have a Unique Selling Point

That's the thing that separates you from any and everyone else. You can do similar things that others are doing, but you must separate yourself to become a success. Don't over think this either; your unique selling point is the exceptional quality that makes you stand out and attract followers, income and helps add value to your market. It's like your signature, everyone has one, and yours is unique to you!

Master Your Craft

Everyone can do something, but your quality of expertise and experiences will separate you from the rest. Now, this doesn't mean that you shouldn't start until you become an expert. It means you are going to have to study your passion as you go along, figure out what you can do to fill the gap that everyone else is missing, and then (most importantly) MAX OUT that opportunity!!

Consistency is Key

If you want to succeed at ANYTHING in life, you are going to need to be consistent. Consistency shows commitment and dedication, but most people can't do it; especially when there isn't instant gratification. In today's social media age, you must have a consistent flow of content, posts, and videos to feed the audience. Do T.V. networks take a day off? If you want to get through the noise on the internet or anywhere else for that matter, consistency is a must!

People who are working hard to fill the needs and solve the most significant problems of others are often compensated in the most significant ways; not just in financial terms, but also regarding human satisfaction. Desiring to benefit someone other than ourselves is an empowering mindset change, as it shifts the mind from thinking about how we can help ourselves, to how we can help others.

CONNECTING YOUR PASSION WITH PURPOSE

For as long as I can remember, I have been gifted at speaking well; but not always for good. Many of the situations I talked myself into didn't allow me to realize the full potential of my gift. I knew I could convince people to do things, advised a lot of my friends on life and how to handle problems, and my passion was the icing on the cake. When you in the streets finessing women, trying to hustle, and trying to find any way to get over possible. It was hard to see the positive potential in a gift like that, primarily because I wasn't in an environment where that was a regular thing.

I believe in "signs" or little things that occur, signaling to you the probable presence of something else. For example, let's say you play a sport for the first time and you are a lot better naturally than the rest of the players that have been trained; that's a sign that you're talented at that sport. Another example would be thinking you can sing, entering a talent show and getting booed off the stage because your friends lied to you so they wouldn't hurt your feelings. That's a sign that you are not talented at singing. Now, what do you do with those signs?

No one ever told me my ability to speak could be used positively; to communicate with an audience by teaching, storytelling, and providing inspirational support. One of my first signs came when I was in Jr. High school. I wasn't a regular basketball player, but I was athletic, so I tried out and made the team. The season was tough because a lot of the players had played ball in AAU leagues for years, but I had three things that mattered hustle, heart, and motivational support. I didn't play much, but when I got in, I hustled and played with heart, not allowing my lack of skill to affect me. I would yell loud on the bench for my team and always be motivating and inspiring in any way possible; that's why I said motivational support! I was even awarded "most inspirational player" for my role. At the time, I didn't realize that award was a sign. Now, motivational support helps me be successful in working with the youth I serve.

As I look back now, I can tell you plenty of things that were signs telling me to walk into my purpose, but I didn't. It won't happen the exact way we want it to, but it's important to pay attention when life gives you signs that help you create awareness of your strengths, weaknesses, skills, talents or gifts. As the world moves through constant change on many levels, more and more people are feeling called to align their skills and gifts to serve a purpose bigger than themselves or have a sense of contribution. Other examples are emerging in many areas of social change, where people are not giving up their passion for the cause but rather channeling the thing they most love doing in the direction of positive change – and discovering inspired ways to support themselves along the way.

The Ikigai Diagram

Let's look at how passion + purpose = paycheck. The Ikigai diagram below is the one I spoke about early in the chapter. Each of the circles helps contribute to your happiness; all four are crucial to your "reason for being." As we all know, your happiness relies on much more than merely having a career (Vocation) and getting a paycheck (Profession). Likewise, Mission and Passion aren't enough to sustain you financially if you don't know how to turn it into an income stream or business. Your ikigai lies at the center of those interconnecting circles. If you lack in one area, you are missing out on your life's potential. Not only that, but you are missing out on your chance to live a long and happy life.

Take a moment to draw your version of the ikigai diagram and think about the following:

What do you love? What parts of your life bring you peace and make you come alive?

What are you great at? What unique skills do you have that come most naturally to you? What talents have you obtained and what do you excel at even when you aren't trying?

What cause do you believe in? What problem would you solve or makes you want to help? What change would you most love to create in the world? What would you give your life for?

What do people value and pay you for? What service, value or skill do you bring, or could you bring, that delivers real value to others? Something people need and are happy to pay for or share some value in exchange?

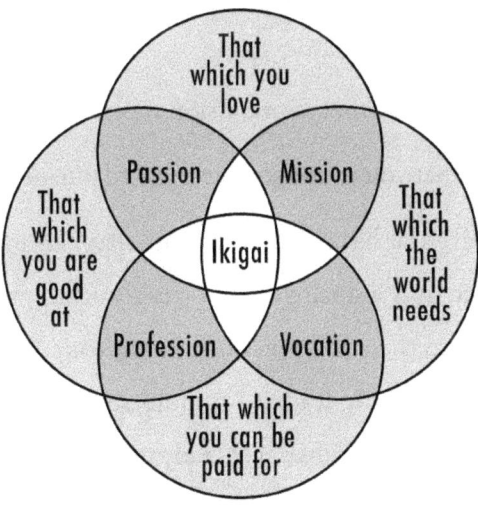

DIAGRAM MADE BY MARK WINN

- **Mission:** What you love
- **Vocation:** What the world needs
- **Profession:** What you can get paid for
- **Passion:** What you're good at
- **Ikigai:** Reason for being

What's stopping you from finding your Ikigai?

Don't you think you can make a career out of your passion?

Can't risk leaving your stable job to pursue your passion?

Do you believe without high levels of education you won't be successful?

Do you believe you have to get permission to follow your dreams?

Have you become too tied up in the daily grind and lost sight of what makes you happy?

Were you told as a child that your passion wasn't a career option?

Are you worried that you're not good enough to pursue your passion?

Every individual has gifts and talents that can make a lasting impact. However, only a small group of people utilize those gifts and talents to live up to their full potential. Tying your gifts and talents to your purpose not only leads to a more successful career but a significant one. Many individuals get ready to retire, like your parents and grandparents, and begin to approach the end of their career looking for a higher significance. The younger generations, are at the other end of their career spectrum but are also looking for relevance right out of the gate. The fact that younger individuals want to have a sense of purpose attached to their careers should give you a hint as to why I wrote this chapter. As a leader, helping others find their passions and helping them have significance in life is becoming a more prominent part of my purpose. I believe that personal development will unlock your potential and develop you into your goal. It's all about learning about yourself, then taking what you learned out to the world and applying it. My passions and mission are to help people find theirs and help them develop to live the life they deserve.

Your purpose is the calling you have in life or reason you were created. Everything you have experienced and will experience in life is for a reason, but you have to figure out what that reason is while simultaneously having purpose related life experiences. Is that confusing? It should be! Identifying your reason for being is not a simple process, but if you can understand that we have a higher purpose than what we might think, then you have a choice on whether you want to pursue it or not. Most individuals could care less about this and focus on comfort and survival. They die without knowing or living their purpose. I believe everyone has a purpose in life and that they can choose to pursue it at any time. The problem is society doesn't talk about this much, so we don't value it as much as we should. Now, this is just my opinion, but it made a life-changing difference for me, and I know it can for you too.

Your passion is an intense desire, emotion, or enthusiasm for something. One way to describe it is a mix of love and hate, you may love something so much you hate to go without it, or you may hate something so much that you would like to change it. We all have passion in life.

When I explain my passion to people when I speak, I always relate it to the Olympic torch. First off, it doesn't go out! No rain or wind puts that torch out. It burns the entire Olympic games. Now imagine your passion is that torch and it burns throughout your whole life. The pain or discomfort in our lives is the fuel for keeping it lit. Adversity needs to be the reason you keep going no matter. Whatever you're already going through is only preparing you for your purpose. When you align yourself to impact other lives and find out how to do that for the rest of your life with intent, integrity and drive that's purpose.

My life completely changed when I found real passions to chase and enjoy in life. I used to pursue things that were meaningless and had no real value; then one night while in prison staring at the wall in my cell, I realized I didn't know myself. I thought about what mattered to me, not what I had been programmed through society and my negative influences to believe mattered. You must release your mind from the chains of following and become an individual.

Anyone who has been successful at this formula has developed a unique selling point. It's easier being you; you don't have to try as hard!

I held the belief that I wasn't supposed to be comfortable doing things outside of the typical stereotypes for a young black man until I was 21 years old. I didn't truly embrace who I was and that I didn't have to be like everyone around me to fit in or be accepted. It was when I got out of my comfort zone, became an individual, developed my gifts to align with my passion, connected that passion to my purpose and started living it, that I became both successful and happy. Now I own who I am, and have been able to identify what I would do if I didn't get paid because I unknowingly did it for two years before the paychecks started coming in.

I tap dance out of bed now because what I'm doing creates income but doesn't feel like work. It's something that isn't motivated solely by money. My philosophy is "impact over income;" meaning I focus on the impact I can make or value I can provide more than the money that I can make. When you develop your skills more to make an impact than an income, the monetary reward will follow you like the Beyhive follows Beyoncé.

I'm not saying this because I read it in a book; I made it happen. I'm a living example. I have no degree, and I'm a felon but managed to develop skills in youth development, start a business from my passion and get a contract with a school district that now has my programs in 3 of their high schools. This passion came from not having a mentor or someone who looked like me and that related to me inside my school. Now I have an opportunity to do it for other youth who need it. The crazy part is I get paid more money than I ever did in a year doing anything, and all from following my passion until it connected with my purpose.

I'm also successful at being a fatherless, full custody father. My father left when I was just 18 months old. Statistics said that I would do the same to my son. The figures were wrong. Coming out of prison I decided to be a part of my son's life full-time like I should. I wasn't going to walk away from my son the way my father walked away from me.

Both of these examples are of situations where I didn't obtain my reward up front. I ran off of sheer passion for something. I had been doing youth development 3 ½ years before a paid contract happened and fought for my son for almost a year before I won custody of him. Only passion kept me on the journey to both!

Everyone deserves the opportunity to live a life of fulfillment and passion. Looking deeply inside yourself and removing all obstacles (real and perceived), can help on your road to finding your career passion, achieving career success, and living your best life.

> When you catch a glimpse of your potential, that is when passion is born.
>
> —Zig Ziglar.

04 LEADERSHIP IS BEHAVIOR, NOT POSITION

> *"A true leader has the confidence to stand alone, the courage to make tough decisions, and the compassion to listen to the needs of others. He does not set out to be a leader, but becomes one by the quality of his actions and the integrity of his intent."*
>
> **Douglas MacArthur**

I believe everyone has leadership qualities. For most people, the tricky part is realizing they are a leader. It starts with self-awareness, direction, and purpose. Leadership is about leading, not being a boss of people. Great leaders lead by example.

Characteristics of a Leader

Being a servant

Taking responsibility

Being a problem solver

Having vision

Finding ways to add value

Leaders see gaps and fill them. Leadership is about having vision, not just sight. When you're a leader, you can see things others can't, and you're able to lead others towards filling that gap. If you can see it, you can do it. There are so many stories of people doing extraordinary things just by creating or having a vision and then leading a group of people who can make that vision a reality.

Some of us worry about the influence we have on people when we don't even have a direction to take them in. I did this for years, and it always produced negative results. In the end, whatever and wherever I was leading them to fell apart, and I accomplished nothing.

Most leaders are defined by being in the front of the pack, but leaders play many roles. The most important function of a leader is to follow. Once you master that role, you can start to develop more characteristics of a leader. I have always taken responsibility for my actions, I have always been a problem solver, and I have always led by example, but I haven't always been fully aware of what I was leading others to or where. Until I learned what a leader indeed is and how I am one, I wasn't instrumental.

I want to share with you the nine styles of leadership. Everyone is a leader and uses their power differently. The roles of a leader might sound the same, but the manner in which they are used is different. I believe that knowing these styles will help you identify the style of leadership you possess and naturally use in your life.

1. **Transformational Leadership**

Inspires individuals to achieve things they didn't think were possible. Leading by example is a stable characteristic of this style, along with building a rapport, being inspirational and having empathy to engage with followers.

2. **Transactional Leadership**

Values order and structure. The focus is on getting results. Usually has formal authority and responsibility in groups or organizations.

3. **Servant Leadership**

Servant leadership places the needs of others as a top priority. Identifies complex problems and finds solutions for them. Being constructive, persistent and motivating are all qualities of this style of leadership.

4. **Autocratic Leadership**

   One person usually makes all the decisions and doesn't accept input from others; they are a dictator. Discipline, preparation, and victory are essential. This style makes typically bad choices based on their ideas and rarely accepting advice from others.

5. **Laissez-faire Leadership**

   Focused on delegating leadership to the ones doing the work. Doesn't need to be in charge of everything. Even though they aren't in power, they still take responsibility for decisions and actions.

6. **Democratic Leadership**

   Democratic leadership places a more participative role in the decision-making process for the group members, while still offering guidance and control to the group. Democratic leadership is one of the most effective styles of leadership.

7. **Bureaucratic Leadership**

   Relies on rules and regulations within a group or organization to lead. Stepping out of the role can be difficult and make them less useful. Bureaucratic leadership was used by some of the first world rulers and is one of the oldest styles of leadership.

8. **Charismatic Leadership**

   Uses charm and persuasiveness to lead. This style of leadership is driven by convictions and commitment to the cause it leads. People with this leadership style are great communicators and are sometimes mistaken for the transformational leader. The differences between the two are focus and audience.

9. Situational Leadership

Situational Leadership is a style that adapts to the existing and changing needs of a group or organization. The leader must have the insight to switch their leadership strategy to suit the constant changes. This type of leadership is the most common style.

Shoes that are one size don't fit everyone, and neither does one style of leadership. Using one technique will not always be the most effective and could affect your ability to lead. I believe everyone can harness multiple leadership styles, and some have already taken advantage of this ability. Utilizing different leadership styles separates a good leader from a great leader. Great leaders have an instinct and understand what needs to be done, along with the people they are leading. Most environments are ever-changing, and to be most effective for the benefit of your group, team, or organization, you must realize that it takes more than one leadership style.

Section 1
BECOMING AN EFFECTIVE LEADER: MY BIGGEST TEST

The most significant test of leadership in my life was becoming a father, and one with full custody and single at that. Growing up not knowing my dad caused me to harbor a lot of resentment, and I had many issues because of it. The odds were against me; I was a felon, had only been released from prison a year before and didn't have a clue as to how to even begin being a father.

Instead of being negative, blaming others, and making excuses for not solving my problems, however, I stepped up to the challenge. During my custody battle, I represented myself with no lawyer. It was difficult learning how things worked legally, but I refused to give up. I had to serve a more significant purpose and become what my father wasn't to me. This decision changed my life forever!!!

This chapter uses my own experiences as examples of leadership. I hope that it has helped you understand how to become a leader even when you are lost, in trouble and unsure how to be a leader. When I finally learned how to be one, it wasn't just a word anymore; it was a way of life. I began to realize that most of the people I looked up to had leadership qualities too. It only made sense to make this an essential principle of my life. I didn't grow up with a lot of positive influences at home, in the streets or at school. Since you're reading this book, it's highly likely that the same can be said about you. Negative influences, however, are everywhere; but that shouldn't stop you from becoming a leader. It didn't stop me. Once I learned how to use my leadership qualities, I capitalized on them by transferring skills acquired from past experiences to my present and taking them to the next level.

Although it may not seem like it to most, my going t to prison was a huge step towards becoming a leader and maintaining the leadership that I had always possessed. For example, when I chose not to "snitch," or tell on other people while in court, I was taking responsibility for my actions.

When you choose to do or not do something, you must be willing to take responsibility regardless of the outcome. When you blame others, you are giving up power, and leadership is only maintained when you retain the ability to lead. Concentrate on what you have control of, and don't ever give anyone or anything power over your life by giving them responsibility for your actions. You can control 90% of your life; the other 10% we can't control, let it go!

Instead of wasting time blaming others or playing the victim, figure out how to overcome the obstacles life places in front of you; never depend on others to rescue you from your problems. How can you lead others when you don't participate in your rescue? You will face many challenges in life; part of leadership is solving them for yourself as well as others.

> *Who we are cannot be separated from where we're from.*
>
> —Malcom Galdwell

05 SKILL DEVELOPMENT

I write this chapter for the dedicated and ambitious individuals who want more from their skills; the person who doesn't want to work a 9-5 forever; the inspiring professional who wants to take the industry by storm, and the passionate, creative individuals who want to take control of their value.

I worked hard to figure out how I could avoid doing what I didn't want to do (work for someone else) and still make money that allowed me to pay my bills, position myself for more opportunities and live a better lifestyle through my efforts. I read books, watched videos, and I studied successful people who enjoyed what they did and did it at a high level or were aspiring to do so. The one thing I discovered that was consistent with each person was that they were an expert or very knowledgeable about whatever they were good at or passionate about.

I write that to say that if you take any advice from me take this, one thing that made me change my whole view on life was seeing people develop skills around things they were passionate about; that provided them opportunities doing things for themselves that they loved, and in places they never imagined. These people received their value in exchange for their level of skill. It doesn't matter what skill level you have either; you can acquire value in exchange for it.

We will get more into the different skill levels below. I'm not telling you to become an expert if you don't want to, but what I am telling you is that you can, and I want to explain how it can benefit you. How about we start with how it has benefited me.

Whatever skills you hope to develop, learning new things takes practice, practice and yes, more practice. Whether it's learning to play an instrument, a sport or how to manage your life, there are four levels one must journey through during skill development. The goal is to reach the final level - "Master"–someone who does not have to think about the activity that they're very good at; their craft comes naturally to them. You see it in athletes and entertainers all the time; individuals who have dedicated so much time to something that they make it look easy, yet it seems almost impossible for an average everyday person.

Section 1
EXPERTISE

An expert is someone who has substantial experience through practice and education in a specific field. The knowledge can be self-taught or learned in school through a curriculum. There are plenty of examples of both educational styles working; even combining them can help develop expertise. My advice is to become an expert at your passion. When you focus on something that is genuinely interesting to you, it's easier to overcome obstacles, solve problems, and have a desire to succeed at a high level. My passion has helped me enjoy the process of learning, applying, and doing necessary tasks even when I don't feel like doing them.

Now, most people aren't able to put in the time, effort, and consistency it takes to become an expert at something without being forced too. Which means it's usually for someone else's benefit and doing something they don't enjoy. I want to empower you to put the time into yourself, on something that will benefit you. Now it's not a bad thing for it to help someone else but this book is all about personally developing yourself. I want you to have control of your value by becoming an expert. Remember you can become an expert in anything you choose to put the time into. No matter what you become an expert in, it's important to understand you are valuable. You can go any route you want with it, but make sure that if you start it, you go all in or don't do it at all.

The reason I share this is that a lot of people have a hard time working with others or finding purpose in the work they do. I had an issue working for someone else. I wanted to be in control of my destiny and find a way to do it without selling drugs or robbing people. I had a work ethic and didn't have a problem working, but I did have a problem with the kind of work I was doing, e.g., construction, general labor, and dead-end jobs. The crazy part is I knew I had a problem. I could not stand to work for other people, and I think it's a condition; "Entrepreneurs Disease" (ED). I didn't like someone else telling me what to do, having my job affected because a co-worker wasn't doing theirs, and overall, just not having control and ownership while feeling invaluable made me miserable. Please don't forget I'm a felon, so jobs didn't come as easy with a criminal record either. All of these realizations soon led me to entrepreneurship, and at first, I failed miserably, but I learned so much in the process. I then took what I learned from my failures and applied it to start my own business providing youth development services.

I wrote this chapter to help you understand that you aren't alone. The problem is you don't always have someone to help you through this process so it haunts you and you live unhappily. I didn't hate work. I just hated doing it for other people. I wanted to create something and have ownership. I wanted my efforts to be valued and my fate to be determined by my own decisions. I think that's one of the benefits of owning a company; having the freedom to choose. I am not saying that having a job is wrong or that you don't have to have one to get where you're going, but if you can slowly change your mindset and actions, you'll find that there may be a much more rewarding and fitting alternative.

Section 2
THE PROCESS

In the book Outliers: The Story of Success, Malcolm Gladwell studied the most successful people in the world, sports athletes, entrepreneurs, entertainers, and scientists, to understand what they had in common with their successes. They weren't successful just because they were smart or had talent; being smart or talented doesn't guarantee success, or in this case, make you an expert. In fact, a lot of it was hard work! Roughly 10,000 hours of it, which is 3 ½ hours every day, for seven years and eight months.

In 1989 John Hayes discovered what is now called the "ten-year rule." Experts often speak of the "ten-year rule," which states that it takes at least a decade of hard work, patience and striving to become highly successful in most endeavors. The "ten-year rule" is related to the idea that it takes about 10,000 hours of practice at something to become an expert. Now don't get me wrong, talent and being smart can give you an advantage. These things will provide you with an edge on others, until a certain point; then deliberate practice becomes the key to maintaining that edge. Remember, hard work beats talent when talent doesn't work hard!

Even the best artists and athletes practice consistently. For example, the most decorated Olympian ever, Michael Phelps, trained six hours a day, six days a week and consumed 12,000 calories every day. He competed in the Olympics and broke almost every record possible.

No one gets a free pass on practice. There are a lot of people who think greatness comes from natural talent, but that's not true.

If you look at the people you look up to, from your parents to your favorite sports players, celebrities, etc., you will see a pattern appear; they each spent crazy amounts of time acquiring the skills necessary to be in the position they are in and have the qualities you admire about them.

I will say this though, the 10,000 hours rule does not, I repeat does not guarantee you success. Having an understanding of this fact will also help you understand the amount of time, effort, and consistency it takes to maximize your potential. Using the 10,000 hours idea is a simple way to help you comprehend the commitment and dedication necessary to operate at a high level. There are a lot of ingredients in the recipe for your success. The most confusing part to most people about success is thinking your recipe is the same as someone else's because you have similar paths. You won't ever have all the same ingredients as someone else, and that's something you can't control, but what you can control is the amount of time you put into your skills.

> *"You might be smarter, your family may come from privilege, your daddy might own a company, but you will not outwork me!"*
>
> **Eric Thomas**

Let's talk about this "recipe for success." We all know everybody cooks their gumbo, makes their potato salad, and bbq's differently; this also applies to life. You didn't grow up with the same privileges or disadvantages as others. The one thing that out weights all of that is the amount of skill or value you have to offer the world. You can look at examples of success, and you will notice that no matter what ingredients they had, what determined the success was the amount of time they put into making what they wanted to happen, happen. All of that time spent created a high level of skill that sustained their success for long periods of time and at a higher level than others.

People are paid for the amount of value they bring to the table. As an apprentice or amateur, you still provide value even though you haven't mastered your skill. You can earn while you learn, it just won't be as much as you'll make once you become an expert. Your skill level starting out is far less important than the time and effort you spend every day to increase that skill level. Practice will help you apply what you are learning through repetition, which gives you an opportunity to develop your skills and your potential further. Experience is the best teacher, and learning while applying what you've learned is one way to speed up your learning curve, which I will talk more about later in this chapter.

Embrace whatever it is that you want to chase and create a future designed by you. I know that you might have to work a job to get the bills paid, attend college to obtain a better education, etc., but one thing I will say is that sacrifice is inevitable to get where you want to be. Just focus on putting in the time and stay focused on building foundational skills and everything else will align itself with your efforts.

In many ways, this law of 10,000 hours is impressive. It means "success'" isn't just about genetics, class or ethnicity; it's not about where you come from or who you know. The only thing that matters is how many hours you've logged developing your craft. I remember this story of a woman who approached a famous singer after he had performed one of his concerts. Making her way to the singer, the woman said, "Sir, I would give my life to sing as you sing." The singer replied, "Ma'am. I did."

Remember, just because you log hours, doesn't automatically mean you become successful. It's not the overall determining factor of your success but will help regarding the following:

Competition

Work Ethic

Skill Development

Experience

Depending on what you are pursuing, there's a lot more that goes into becoming successful. I do, however, believe it's inevitable that we understand both the amount of work it takes to become an expert or the best at something, and how it will separate you from the average individual who is interested but not committed. Elevation requires separation, and the best way to acquire both is by becoming an expert at your craft.

6 Tips to Go from Novice to Expert

1. Deliberate practice requires an environment and method that gives feedback that provides more training designed to help the learner improve his or her performance.

2. Practice must be done near maximal effort, where you're consistently being taken out of your comfort zone. It shouldn't be easy or "fun." Discomfort is where a true potential is found, and skill is developed.

3. The practice must be well defined with specific goals and not aimed at just getting better.

4. You must give the practice your full attention; no playing games; it's all gas, no break.

5. You need feedback and to be continually improving (kaizen), adjusting your efforts in response to the feedback.

6. You must be focused on building and improving specific skills by breaking them down and concentrating on aspects of those skills and developing them progressively over time.

Section 3
LEVELS TO THIS….

If you know Meek Millz, then you know that there are "levels" to this life. If you don't know him, maybe you can recall playing a game that had skill levels, e.g., beginner, intermediate, pro, etc. There are levels to everything in life, school, work, sports, etc. In this section, we are going to discuss these "levels," and help you understand the importance of each one. It's important to know and understand the process of becoming or doing something at higher levels. No one who has ever indeed sustained or maintained success at any level by skipping through the process to get there.

In my example, we have a diagram that shows us Abraham Maslow's Four Stages (levels) of Learning: The Novice, The Apprentice, The Journeyman, and The Expert/Master. Now everyone has different skill levels, and some people are more advanced than others, but that doesn't mean they can skip levels. In school, you can skip a grade or two maybe, but in life, and when it comes to developing, you have no shortcuts. For example, plenty of all-star athletes dominate at a high level in grade school and college, but when they get to the professional level, most of them realize their skills aren't always as dominating. Even without the experience, a rookie can get into a championship early by dominating, but soon recognize that their talents can only get them so far without experience. Now I know there are exceptions to every rule, but even the people we consider the greatest of all time had to go through the process of leveling up to achieve that greatness.

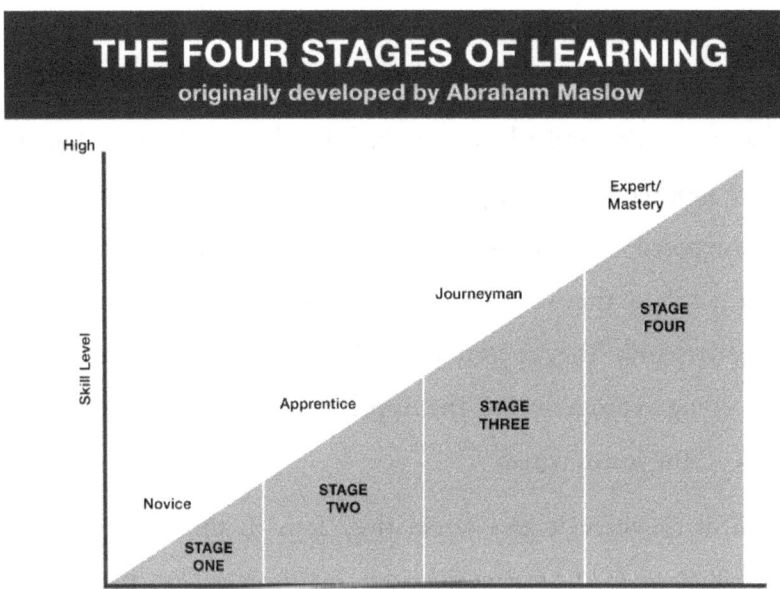

4 STAGES OF LEARNING LEVELS OF EXPERTISE

- **The Novice**

Novices know little or nothing about the work, certainly too small to be able to perform to an acceptable standard. A Novice must be taught (or shown) the basics of what is to be done before they can have any chance of being productive. But, as we all know (and wish were not true sometimes), mastering a craft doesn't happen overnight. Look at "overnight successes" for example. If you do a little research, you will see there is typically year's and year's worth of hard work, mistakes, and failures lurking behind the scenes of their so-called success. Indeed, before learning any skill, we must begin naïve. This is called The Novice stage.

- **The Apprentice**

A novice becomes an apprentice when they can perform jobs and tasks to basic standards. They've had their basic training and now look for more coaching and practice to get better at what they do. As they're exposed to new concepts and skills, they start to realize their limitations. Sure they've picked a few things up, but they still don't fully understand. They're committed though, and they stick with it, and in doing so progress into The Apprentice stage.

- **The Journeyman**

This is where it gets fascinating. It is in the stage of The Journeyman where the real work begins. In this stage: 'Practice (most definitely) makes perfect.' This stage is all about perspiration–the physical and mental struggle on the road to mastery. The amount of concentration and focus necessary will cause mental and physical exhaustion. So while it's a time of great practice, it also requires great patience. Also known as "good days and bad days," a cyclical pattern of 'failure' and 'success' may emerge. But progress is being made, and they are beginning to see the fruits of their labor.

- **Expert**

The Expert operates entirely by intuition. He or she knows what their goal should be, what to do about it, and what should happen as a result. They're emotionally involved and invested in the whole process, and since they're running on intuition, they might have a hard time explaining why they do things to non-experts. An expert can be believed, by having a certain level of credential, training, education, professional status, publication or experience, to have specialized knowledge of a subject beyond that of the average person.

- **The Master**

Masters create new knowledge. They invent new and better ways to do a job, and they can teach others how to do it. They are truly unique individuals and seek to learn in unique and personal ways. With any skill, technique or craft, the ultimate goal is to achieve a point where you are "unconsciously competent." A natural. One could say a "genius." In essence: it is the stage of The Master. You can spot 'Masters' right away. They pick up the guitar, and it's automatic. And not only is it effortless, often there's no thought to it at all. But it takes time. And while some skills in academic or business contexts can take a few months, or weeks even, pure mastery of a complex skill can take much longer.

Section 4
KAIZEN (CONTINUOUS IMPROVEMENT)

Resist the urge to see immediate results and receive short-term payoffs. Instead, build a daily habit of constant improvement to create the compound effect in your life and produce incredible results.

Darren Hardy

The Kaizen philosophy can make it easy to commit to that goal, make those changes in your life, or even acquire skills you didn't have before. You should aim to make progress in life continually. My son and I have a saying, we say, "Try harder to be better," and I have managed to make this apart of his mindset at nine years old.

Instead of aiming for big, extreme changes, what if you pointed to find small changes or actions you can make starting now. Small, simple, continuous actions are the foundation of habits that stick.

Einstein once said, "Compounding is the greatest mathematical discovery of all time."

You can use this strategy for improving your health, relationships, finances, or anything else. The changes are small, almost unnoticeable, and they offer little or no immediate result, no big win, no obvious I-told-you-so payoff.

This is why most people won't ever have real success; they want the microwave, instant success. If you asked the most successful people in any industry what it took to get there, they would say the same thing I'm trying to explain, which is it took continuously improving. Many people don't find success so attractive anymore once they realize how much time it takes to achieve it. It's also easier to just not do it. Imagine if you stay on that diet or stopped that bad habit you have? Doesn't it sound easy? Well, it takes kaizen to accomplish such a feat. You must continuously do an action every day, which results in you improving. The part that most people do well is not doing it at all, because that's a lot easier. Consistency is one of the hardest things for a human being to do. Now don't get me wrong we can be consistent in the things we want to do, but what about the things you don't want to do? The long, laborious process is the only way through. You can't achieve tremendous life success with a quick fix. Nobody gets it that easy.

"Instead of trying to make extreme changes in a short amount of time, make small improvements every day that will slowly lead to the change you want. Each day, focus on getting 1% better in whatever it is you're trying to improve. That's it. Just 1%.

It might not seem like much, but those 1% improvements start compounding on each other. In the beginning, your improvements will be so small as to seem almost unreal. But in time and ever so slowly, you'll start to notice the improvements in your life. It may take months or even years, but the improvements will come if you focus on consistently upping your game by 1%."

The idea of kaizen is that repetitive action is repeatedly done over an extended period. When you focus on the practice instead of the performance, you can enjoy the present moment and improve at the same time.

Besides the fact that I have been living longer, I have experienced a lot of the things in life that helped me to develop the youth I work with. Growing up fatherless, being locked up in juvenile detention, and many other adversities I've faced, have given me a lot of experience that I reverse engineered into skills. This real-life experience helps me relate to young people and possibly help them not make the decisions I have; it empowers them to find their value and give it to the world as I did.

> *"When you improve a little each day, eventually big things occur. When you improve conditioning a little each day, eventually you have a big improvement in conditioning. Not tomorrow, not the next day, but eventually a big gain is made. Don't look for the big, quick improvement. Seek the small improvement one day at a time. That's the only way it happens—and when it happens, it lasts."*
>
> **John Wooden**

Section 5
THE LEARNING CURVE

A learning curve is the rate of a person's progress in gaining experience or new skills, and also the time required to learn specific information, or acquire those skills, etc. Learning should not end after formal education. Lifelong learning, the ongoing, voluntary, and self-motivated pursuit of knowledge, can enrich your life and make you a better person every day. When we talk about learning curves, there are shallow ones and deep ones. A Ph.D. student has a deep learning curve from their associates to there doctoral degree. A kid learning to ride a bike has a shallow learning curve, with not as much information to learn. The easiest thing to remember about developing any skill whether it's basketball, driving, or public speaking, is that it's a curve, not a line.

The first improvements happen fast because your skills are in the beginning stages; for instance, in basketball, the first time someone teaches you how to keep your head up while dribbling down the court, you instantly become three times better than you were. When you're learning to drive, something as basic as learning to use your blinker will mean that your skill skyrockets with that simple information and practice. If it's your first-time public speaking, someone telling you to be authentic might instantly improve your speaking abilities more than anything else you'll ever be taught.

I started to learn a lot of things that helped me progress from worker to owner. I don't think I'm an expert yet, but I'm becoming one. I have been working on my craft for five years. I have developed characteristics through my life experiences that have prepared me to be disciplined enough to gain skills that will help me become an expert in the youth development field. Also, I'm a college student getting my bachelor's degree in youth development from Highline Community College. The amount of time you spend beating on your craft (area of expertise), the faster you can become an expert and gain higher levels of skill. Research agrees, and shows that we retain in memory "10% of what we read, 20% of what we hear, 30% of what we see, 50% of what we hear and see, 70% of what we say, 90% of what we say and do."

I single-handedly increased my learning curve by immersing myself in the process. I started with volunteering which was my novice stage. I learned a lot of skills and information doing the volunteer work. It was a two-year-long process that was a continuous progression toward improvement and knowledge of my profession. Soon I moved up to an apprentice. I started to notice the level up when the staff and community members told me how effective I was with students and in the community. I am working on leveling up to journeyman right now in my career. I have acquired skills, but I'm not outstanding yet.

Section 6
THE IMPORTANCE OF MASTERY

"There is no end to education. It is not enough that you read a book, pass an examination, and get a degree. The whole of life, from the moment you are born to the moment you die, is a process of learning."

— Jiddu Krishnamurti

Becoming a master sounds difficult and can be misleading if you don't understand the process of becoming one. A master is a leader, influencer, or teacher in a particular area. Reaching this level of mastery can involve multiple things, for example, experiences, education, and skills. I know that with hard work, consistency, and continuous improvement we can all become masters in our area of choice, whether it's parenthood, entrepreneurship, professional athletics, etc.

When you have a certain level of knowledge, ability, and you put in the time, you are considered an expert. Mastery can only be attained through the development of in-depth knowledge or skill. It is the highest accomplishment in any craft.

Mastery does not require you to be perfect, but it does require you to pursue perfection. It's not just about the time you put in; it's also about the continuous development of skills. Even becoming a master doesn't mean your successful, you must align yourself with opportunities that will correlate with your skills. Sometimes individuals spend time developing skills that they have no plan to use; they just genuinely enjoy the process of continuous learning.

Pursuing mastery requires a sacrifice – a path quite unlike average attempts at creating something, which can be done during regular working hours or in your free time. If you genuinely want to become the best you can be, then you must actively choose to spend your time there and avoid other pursuits. You must sacrifice for your craft. Mastery is not easy. It is not simple or quick or painless. If you pay your way with effort and sacrifice, mastery will more than pay you back in discovery, fulfillment, and growth. It will teach patience, discipline, how to handle failure, perseverance, and a whole lot about yourself.

They say mastery requires 20,000 hours of practice, which is double the amount of an expert. The secret ingredients are desire and time, which are a lot easier to come by when you are passionate about what you're pursuing. The amount of time it takes is not all it takes. Putting in the dedicated, repetitive practice is only one step. The intellectual abilities of an individual also help speed up this process and help them advance at a faster pace.

The reason I wrote about mastery is that it's not a special position reserved for specific people or a talent you possess at birth. It doesn't matter about any of the things that society has disqualified you from. I want to open your mind to a higher level of thinking that could be used toward helping you reach your maximum potential. We spend years at a job working for someone else, going to college, and ultimately mastering things for ourselves and others. It's important to be conscious of the things we are mastering and how we can use them in many areas to benefit us. A lot of times people don't realize they could use that 20 years of experience from mastering plumbing, being a manager, or cooking for others to start their own business or even use the skills to transfer to other opportunities.

Section 7
PERSONAL MASTERY

Personal mastery is about living life with meaning and purpose. It's knowing where you want to go and how you are going to get there. Personal mastery is the ultimate personal development task! Working on yourself is truly important, and it's essential to invest in that mastery.

I'm on this journey in life trying to obtain personal mastery, but the journey never ends. I choose to become and strive to be the best Shaun Worthy I can be to this world while I'm in it. I want to leave a legacy. I'm not just talking about assets, money, or material things. It's deeper than that; I have a goal to break stigmas, stereotypes, and cycles that have been in my family forever. The only way to do this is to provide an example and be the foundation for my family, friends, and associates. As a man, I want to be remembered for my integrity, work ethic, kind treatment of people, my loyalty, etc. The non-tangible qualities that make me who I am will give all the rest of my legacy value.

THESE ARE THE 9 PILLARS THAT MAKE UP THE FOUNDATION FOR PERSONAL MASTERY.

- **Loving Oneself**

   Knowing yourself is an important part of life, and you can walk in your truth without worry what others think. You have full belief in who you are and what you're capable of, and you have the confidence to express who you are and love every part of it.

- **Self-Discipline**

   One of the most important factors of success is discipline. Personal mastery is about committing to goals and disciplining yourself to accomplish them; continually training yourself to be obedient to the commitments.

- **Proactive Behavior**

   You understand who you are and where you are going. When you learn to be proactive with your behavior, you can problem solve solutions and overcome adversity without just reacting.

- **Contribution to Others**

   We have an obligation to contribute back to our communities and others that we choose to serve. It's important to understand how we impact others lives and take steps towards achieving that impact no matter what the size.

- **Positive Attitude**

   The right mentality is an integral part of personal mastery. You have to have the right mental attitude to make decisions and take action in life. Personal mastery is about turning negative energy into positive energy, shaping your thoughts, and thinking positively and powerfully.

- **Overcoming Fears**

   Without understanding our fears and taking steps to overcome them, we limit ourselves from reaching our fullest potential. The goal is to reshape our thinking to accept challenges as opportunities. Personal mastery takes away fear and eliminates any self-limiting beliefs we have in life.

- **Achieving Success**

   The process of achieving personal mastery helps you create success in whatever you choose to pursue. When you start to understand the value of personal mastery truly, your success will accelerate.

- **Absolute Happiness**

    One of the most important goals in life is to be happy. The journey towards personal mastery is about finding what that is and living it out on a daily basis.

- **Opportunity for Growth**

    We must grow through what we go through. When we start to look at challenges as opportunities instead of a negative situation, we can learn valuable lessons. Personal mastery is the process of continuous growth and learning that come from opportunities that look like adversity.

    Personal mastery is about creating your own life and determining your destiny. It's the journey towards understanding yourself, knowing where you want to go, and continually learning and developing so you achieve absolute happiness, success, and life fulfillment.

Section 8
INTENSE DEDICATION & OBSESSION

Those who are experts or masters become extremely dedicated to it. It's hard to reach this position, and it won't become real without intense dedication. If you want to achieve your goals, dreams, and aspirations, you must think about it all the time. Think of different ways to improve yourself or different ways to reach your goals.

Start obsessing about it. Don't focus on anything else. As Michael Jordan once said, "In order to excel, you must be completely dedicated to your chosen sport."

"I'm hungry for knowledge. The whole point is to learn every day; to get brighter and brighter. That's what this world is about. You look at someone like Gandhi, and he glowed. Martin Luther King glowed. Muhammad Ali glows. I think that's from being bright all the time and trying to be brighter." Jay-Z

Obsession is looked at in a negative mindset and seen as unhealthy. That's not entirely true though; there is such a thing as having definite obsessions, which is what you see in experts, masters, and other unique individuals. They made their one thing (passion) their obsession.

It makes more sense to create a life from a real passion that flows from personal choices about your purpose in life than to live average and less satisfying "normal" lives that produce unhappiness and boredom.

Becoming an expert and master is about dominating your space, and we all have an area in life we can dominate; whether it is video games, knitting, or anything else. You can develop a need or value for skills you already have. If you plug this information into the information from chapter 1, you will see that designing your life is possible.

> *"Only one who devotes himself to a cause with his whole strength and soul can be a true master. For this reason, mastery demands all of a person."*
>
> **Albert Einstein**

Section 9
TRANSFERABLE SKILLS

Transferable skills are skills and abilities that are relevant and helpful to different areas of life: socially, professionally, and at school.

Your whole life you have been learning and experiencing things that helped you acquire skills. While you may or may not have a lot of work experience at this stage in the game, you likely have more transferable skills than you realize.

These skills can come from all kinds of places like school, sports, your home, and the experiences you have. They are life skills and will continue to develop. When you can add these skills to your passion, expertise, and overall life it gives you an advantage that is almost natural. Many times developing these skills occurs through the repetitive tasks that you must complete or the requirements to fix, solve, and adapt to things. When you have skills, whether they're rare or basic, you can bring value to someone or something. Each person has transferable skills, and we must be aware of how they can benefit us in multiple ways.

Section 10
FINDING MENTORSHIP

Another important task is finding a mentor. Why do you need one? Well, because no one has ever done it alone. Someone taught them, helped them, and even groomed them into who they are. When you have a mentor, they add value to your life, have a similar interest, and have reached a level of success.

Mentors can have a personal relationship with you, or it can be an individual that you follow on TV, Social Media, etc. You don't need to know them personally, and they don't have to be alive. Find someone who does what you want to do, has characteristics that you find unique, and that has reached some success. Then, take out a notebook and start to write down notes from interviews, songs, books, and any other content you can find. You will learn that success leaves clues, and you must discover those clues from people who are already experiencing or have already experienced success. You may also have more than one mentor; this is very common. A mentor is not someone who tells you what to do, but more a guide that provides information and support. Remember this; you have to find what's valuable to your development. Not everything your mentor says or has experienced will fit into your life.

I dedicated my life to entrepreneurship, speaking, and youth development. No, I'm not an expert or master yet! I am putting in my 10,000 - 20,000 hours just like I'm telling you to do.

I wrote this chapter to share with you how my potential unlocked another level when I learned about becoming an expert and developing skills; I hope that these nuggets of information will help you too. Just remember you have a choice and can choose to be whatever you want. My advice is to determine your passion and start now!

> *The happiness of a human in this life does not consist in the absence but in the mastery of their passion.*
>
> **Alfred Tennyson**

> *Be miserable or motivate yourself. Whatever has to be done, is your choice.*
>
> —Wayne Dyer

06 THE LION & THE GAZELLE

> *"Every morning in Africa, a gazelle wakes up, it knows it must outrun the fastest lion, or it will be killed. Every morning in Africa, a lion wakes up. It knows it must run faster than the slowest gazelle, or it will starve."*
>
> **African Proverb**

You have a choice!

You can be the Lion, and your goals the Gazelle.

Or

You can be the Gazelle, and the Lion is your life.

Entirely different forces motivate these two creatures. And their attitudes determine their outcomes. The gazelle is reactive. It grazes the land, going about its day with no particular plan. The grass is abundant, so it's not desperate for food.

There's no motivation to do anything. The gazelle has no "why." But then, the lion comes.

The lion is proactive because it already has a "why." The lion knows if it doesn't kill the gazelle, then not only will it not eat, the family doesn't either. A lion may or may not always feel like chasing a gazelle for hours or sometimes days at a time before eating, but the decision is straightforward; either it does, or it doesn't. If it doesn't, however, then it knows what that means.

I believe that you can be either the lion or the gazelle in life. Now think about it. Which one are you…?

Do you tell everyone you want to make changes, start something new, or improve a particular area of your life — but you act like a gazelle? Are you waiting for things to happen to you? Do you think things are going to develop, create, and build themselves? If so, you don't have an unstoppable "WHY." You're not hungry. You're just "kind of motivated." You want an appetizer, not a full meal. You're not behaving like a lion because you don't feel like there are any real reasons to attack life.

I have news for you. You're no longer safe. This is now life or death. So, either get out there and hunt or be hunted by something that makes you its goal. When you aren't "hunting" to achieve, grow, and be fulfilled by accomplishing your goals in life, you are becoming a goal yourself. Like the gazelle, you are waiting and wishing for things to happen a certain way before you move.

I remember hearing Eric Thomas use this African proverb in one of his speeches. It's incredible how much it applied to my life. I want to explain how this became a principle I used to attack life, reach goals, and develop an animal like instinct to live up to my maximum potential.

When I got out of prison, I had only one goal; stay out of prison. I didn't have ambition. I was like that gazelle; just happy to be home, comfortable, and fed. I didn't think about the lion waiting for me in the bushes. For myself, the lion in the bushes included bills, a child in need of a provider, settling for living beneath my full potential, and much, much more.

Instead of staying a gazelle, I started to apply the same energy I had doing negative things, towards doing positive things like setting and reaching goals, hunting my life's purpose, and making it an instinct to take control of my life.

I have entirely changed my present and future by living my life as a lion. I took my adversity and made it my strength. I set a goal to be better than my father, and I broke cycles that have been haunting my family for generations.

Section 1
WHY DO I NEED A WHY?

Until I had a reason to care, I didn't care to have a reason. Everyone's "WHY" will be different, but everyone needs one. What do you get up for every day; is it your family, a burning desire, or another reason that's so personal it becomes a must that you accomplish it? Determining your "why" isn't always easy. It's something that ignites the fire within you, making you an inferno. When you don't have one, you must do some soul searching and evaluate what's important to you. If you don't have a force that drives you, which is what we call a "WHY," then when times get tough you will have nothing to push you through them. It's hard to stay determined when you don't have a reason. You may already have multiple reasons why or develop them through the process of your journey.

Your why is the thing that motivates you to get up every morning and work a little harder to get a little better. It's the thing that pushes you even on the days when all you want to do is pull the covers over your head and hide from everything. Your "why" may change throughout your life, as you get married, start a family, have to care for aging parents, etc., but the questions you have to ask yourself to stay focused on it and overcome all the obstacles you will undoubtedly face, remain mostly the same.

If you've ever faced a significant crisis in your life, you have experienced the power of purpose to tap into the energy, determination, and courage you likely didn't know you had. A clear sense of purpose enables you to focus your efforts on what matters most, compelling you to take risks and push forward regardless of the odds or obstacles.

Section 2
INTRINSIC & EXTRINSIC MOTIVATION

As I was writing, I was thinking a lot about the motivation that the lion has to catch the gazelle. It isn't just a selfish need to kill something. There is an internal motivation that turns into willpower. The lion's family depends on the lion; that's an internal motivational force.

Intrinsic motivation involves engaging in a behavior because it is personally rewarding; essentially, performing an activity for its own sake rather than the desire for some external reward. Extrinsic motivation occurs when we are motivated to perform a behavior or engage in an activity to earn a reward or avoid punishment.

Examples of extrinsic motivation are:
- Studying to get good grades
- Cleaning your room to avoid being punished by your parents
- Playing in a sport to win awards

- Working hard for materialistic things such as cars, houses, etc.

In these examples, the behavior is motivated by a desire to gain a reward or avoid an adverse outcome.

Examples of intrinsic motivation are:

- Playing in a sport because you find the activity enjoyable
- Solving problems because you find the challenge fun and exciting
- Helping people who are less fortunate
- Breaking a cycle in your family, because you don't want to be the same

In these examples, the behavior is motivated by an internal desire to participate in an activity for its own sake.

The difference between the two types of motivation is that extrinsic motivation comes from outside of the individual, while intrinsic motivation comes from within.

I know for a fact that these two behaviors are needed, but I think when you understand that some people don't have an internal desire to engage with a certain thing like school, working out, a job, etc., sometimes it takes extrinsic rewards to build that intrinsic motivation. I'm personally more of an intrinsically motivated individual. Don't get me wrong; I do like material things and rewards. I just know that you will not always have those things as a motivator, or if you do, it might not be enough to drive you. I don't think most people have a clear understanding of what this is or how it motivates them.

The exciting part is, if we use these two behaviors as a tool and resource, we can find ways to accomplish goals, break habits, and overcome challenges.

Just remember that motivation of any type is not going to last long. The goal is to build discipline so that when the motivation wears off, you still have something to stand on and keep you going. You can be motivated, but when you're not, what's going to carry you if not discipline? Motivation doesn't last long; it eventually wears off like cologne.

Section 3
GOALS

Goals are the oxygen for our dreams. It's essential that you realize the significance and importance of goal-setting and apply this knowledge in your life. So, I know this isn't the first time you've heard about the importance of goals, and it's not going to be the last. A goal is a statement written down to achieve an estimated result at a given point in time. Unfortunately, only 3% of Americans have written goals. Those that have them are typically the most successful people.

You wake up every day with a chance to live out your dreams through the goals you set out to accomplish and direct your future by achieving them.

You can predict an enormous part of your life by setting goals and committing to reaching them one by one. The road won't be smooth, and you need to develop some "stick-to-it-iveness" to overcome the adversities and barriers that will come up.

These are some examples of goals:

1. Graduate from college with a 3.0 or higher, by June 2024
2. Save 3,000 dollars to buy a car August 18th, 2018
3. Create a YouTube channel with 10,000 subscribers by Dec 31, 2019
4. Make 100,000 dollars in a year 1/10/19
5. Buy a home 3/9/21

Just imagine your life like the lions. If the lion doesn't reach his GOAL, the gazelle, then the lion or his family doesn't eat. You have to "kill" your goals, or your family doesn't eat. Changing everything that you don't like about your life and your circumstances depends on you accomplishing those goals. Plenty of us have situations or struggles we face in life, and the only thing that determines us getting out of those are the goals we set and whether or not we take action to accomplish them!

My life at one point had only one goal which was to stay out of prison. I didn't have any idea of how to even think about my life. I didn't have too many people in my circle who talked about goals. If they did it was to play college sports or something similar, but with no plans as to how to make it happen. At least I didn't hear any! I started to read a lot of books when I was in prison; most of them were about personal development. Every single one talked about the importance of setting goals, having a plan, and executing the plan.

I started making goals and just finding ways to work towards them without having all the resources. One of my goals was to be a better father to my son, so the easiest way I thought I could make that happen in my position was to develop myself. I started to do little things that over time got me to the goal of being a full custody father. I didn't have that as my goal at first though. It was something that happened from my development into the father I am today. Then I started thinking "What else can I do?" My mind went from 0-100 real quick, and I began to think about things that gave me the vision to become who I am now. I started asking myself "How can I get to that place? I decided to look at the goal and break it down into smaller goals to reach the bigger one. Then I started seeing opportunities, began to plan, and eventually my vision started to appear. Now that vision is a reality that I'm working towards making a legacy.

We all have dreams in this world, and by writing your goals down, you are creating a plan to achieve them step by step. Setting goals also help you live a fulfilled life, by your design and void of the lack of happiness you may be experiencing by having to do what others want you to do. Many people never accomplish a single goal in life, and some settle for a more accessible route. If you think trying is risky, wait till you get the bill for not trying.

Section 4
THE IMPORTANCE OF HAVING VISION ATTACHED TO YOUR GOALS

The great thing about vision is, once you have it, you will slowly detach from people who don't fit into your vision, and you will align yourself with people who do. No one will be able to fulfill their purpose alone, because their purpose is more prominent than themselves and that is the intended purpose! The great thing about purpose is, it will not only benefit and help you, but it will also make room for other people to learn and grow in your purpose and your vision as well. A vision is a picture or an idea you have in your mind about your business, education, or anything else that you want to happen. A clear vision helps you pursue your dreams and achieve your goals. A vision that is clear will open your mind to the limitless possibilities of your future.

It will help you to overcome challenges that will get in the way and enables you to hold on when times are difficult. A vision that is well defined helps you to focus and create a purpose. If you do not have an idea of who you want to be, how you want to succeed or what you want out of life, you will begin to lack drive, and your life becomes a sequence of random events.

A strong vision connects with your passions and greatest potentials. Regardless of what is going on in the world or challenges that present themselves, a vision helps you know what and why you are doing the things you are doing. Having vision is most important on the path to your success in life. You feel much more valuable as a person when you set and achieve visions and goals.

Vision is used for two different things: inspiration and prediction. It is first applied to inspire you in reaching something that you want. It is also used to predict changes in the future and interests you have.

A vision might be the most powerful way to keep you focused on what you want in life while keeping you motivated in achieving it. It will open up your mind to many possibilities and a brighter and bigger future. When you can envision a future that is better, happier, more productive, you are more likely to make the changes that are necessary for you to reach that type of life.

When a leader has a vision, they can see today as it is and determine a future that grows and improves. A successful leader can see the future and still stay focused in the present. For a successful leader, a vision is not seen as a dream, but a reality that has not come into existence. Leaders readily perceive a vision because their dedication and confidence are powerful. Leaders can spend hours upon hours to bring their visions forth. Their vision acts as a force within them, driving them to action.

A vision is a potent force in anyone's life, but a vision is essential in unlocking your full potential. The continual presence of a vision helps to motivate against forces of resistance: failure, emotional hardships (negative feedback) and other struggles.

When you create a successful vision, you begin to feel passionate about it. The only way to be successful in your vision is to visualize it and set goals and a plan of action to reach it. Over time, you will begin to see more and more of your vision becoming a reality until one day you are living your vision.

A vision is the capability to see beyond your current reality, creating and inventing what does not now exist and becoming what you are not right now. A vision is essential to all aspects of life. Building your vision does not have to be difficult as long as you know what it is you see for yourself in the future.

Section 5
INTERESTED VS COMMITTED

There is a big difference between being interested and being committed. I think a lot of individuals would make better decisions based on knowing this information. When you're interested, you will do it when it's convenient or comfortable. When you're committed to something, you accept no excuses, only outcomes. There is something deep inside of you that wills you to accomplish everything necessary to become successful; there's a conviction that has a meaning so deep it runs through the veins and makes your heart pump.

I have found that what helps me stay committed is my passion for the outcome. Just thinking about achieving the goal makes me feel excited, and that excitement motivates me to take action. It's no accident that the most successful people in the world are passionate about what they do. They repeatedly have that drive and ambition to take their life forward. Nothing can stop them. It is not that these people are necessarily smarter or talented than anyone else, they just have absolute faith, commitment, and enthusiasm about what they are doing.

Commitment means staying loyal to what you said you were going to do long after the mood you said it in has left. I'm not going to lie; I didn't always feel like writing this book, but I don't like to give up on anything, especially when it's going to help me grow and prosper. There was a desire to do something that no one else in my family had done. Also, I wanted to write this book only having a GED to show people that you don't always have to meet society's "criteria" for being successful to do something you want to do. All of those things lit a flame inside of me that would never go out, and that willed me into action. All commitments start out as an interest or desire to learn or know more about someone or something. You can't just jump into a commitment without first having an interest in it. Once the interest grows due to repeated experiences engaging in an activity, it produces a greater feeling of commitment.

What 100% commitment looks like:

- If you are committed to your goal, then there are no excuses, only results.
- You have discipline – It's just part of your daily practice.
- You don't have to think about it anymore. The decision has been made – you're doing it.
- It's not negotiable.
- You "turn up" every day despite obstacles and not feeling like it; no matter what the circumstances.

What being interested looks like:

- You do it inconsistently – only when you remember or "feel like it."
- You find excuses NOT to do it.
- You wake up each morning fighting the voices in your head over whether to do it today, do it tomorrow, or not do it at all.
- You justify your lack of commitment. "I haven't got the time." "It's not my fault." "I should have…." "I'm too tired." "I deserve a day off."
- You make attempts to start but easily give up.
- You're still doubting the decision even though you've already made it.

- You feel irritated because you know what you should do, but you still don't do it.

My whole life I have struggled to understand what this meant. I didn't have an idea of how being interested versus committed applied to my life or how I could change my circumstances with this information. I used to follow the shiny objects, money, and even other people's dreams. Those things didn't get all my effort though because they didn't mean much. When I started following my passion, I became involved in the commitment to turn it into my reason for living. When I began, it wasn't as strong a desire as it is now. Now everything I do is in alignment with my goals, vision, and passion.

I have no problem sacrificing, failing, and taking responsibility for my success. I am driven by an internal force that creates an ambition to succeed that is naïve to the possibility of failure. All I have to do is be consistent building small disciplines, stay focused on the outcomes, and keep faith in the process. Commitment is the anchor to building the life that you want, and without it, your goals and visions will remain dreams.

I committed to a mission that can't be compromised with interest. You can't fake the funk, or act like your committed for very long. Your actions will tell the truth about the integrity you have involved in the process of making your dreams a reality.

> *A people that value its privileges above its principles soon loses both.*
>
> —Dwight D. Eisenhower

07 PRINCIPLES OVER EMOTIONS

When you identify the things that you value the most and the goals you want to pursue in your personal, professional, and family life, you can use them to create principles. You can develop your values and goals according to these principles, or you can use them to help you realize where your current values, goals, and behaviors are.

If you find that you haven't always been living up to the principles that you want to embrace, you can make meaningful changes to yourself and your goals and values.

Principles can be described as rules or laws that are common. People also make their guiding principles in life. Whenever they are in doubt, they can resort back to these principles, and all doubts are cleared. Having a set of principles is like having a compass on the journey of life when we feel that we are lost or unable to find the right path. One must have clear-cut principles about concepts such as fairness, justice, equality, truthfulness, honesty, etc. Having a belief allows one to have a stand that is a comforting thought. Determine what vision and mission mean for you. When you develop some guidelines for your vision and mission, you create principles in your life.

Principle over emotion is an essential chapter in this book. Let's get straight to the point; you cannot make real decisions based on feelings. I will tell you from experience, I made most of my teenage choices based on emotions, and it didn't work out well for me.

By 18, I was going to prison and having a baby with a young lady I didn't even love. I can say this, no one wants to go to jail, and part of the reason I went was based off emotional decisions. I decided to listen to this little voice called greed, which is why I didn't care about the risks or the possible outcome; even with my son on the way.

Although I made an emotional decision, that doesn't mean I didn't have principles that I stood on. One of which was not being a deadbeat father and making excuses for why I wasn't in my child's life like my dad did.

Being the complete opposite of my father was a burning desire that I know I share with a lot of young men and women who have a parent or parents that have failed them. Not being like him became a principle that I embedded in my life, and whatever you feel as strongly about should become the same for you as well. It might not be your father and doesn't have to be a parent; it can be anyone or anything.

It's very human to operate based on your emotions, and it's also very unproductive. How many times have you run off your emotions and things turned out well? The problem is that because feelings change based on your situation, they aren't reliable.

One primary key to balancing your principles over your emotions is having self-awareness, which is another characteristic you can't buy. The good news is you can become more aware by assessing your actions. It's that simple, but the hard part is being present and honest while adjusting the areas you see fit. This one characteristic is undervalued, and not talked about too much.

Every time we face hard choices, we improve our principles by asking ourselves difficult questions. Emotions change, but beliefs do not. You stay true to your beliefs no matter how you feel, or what the situation is. So, make sure they're things you wholeheartedly believe. Do you already have principles you stand on, and do you live by them?

Yes   or   No

The principles that are most valuable come from your own experiences. The reflections on those experiences will help you mold your beliefs. That doesn't mean you can't create some principles now though; some of it is just common sense and what you already believe or feel. Every person who lives a life of purpose has principles; I challenge you today to add at least six principles to your life.

You might remember me saying I'm a full custody father. Well, I achieved that by making decisions based on principles and not my emotions. It was NOT easy to do. See, one day I was supposed to be getting my son for the week when his mom started acting funny. I had been in prison the first to years of his life, so I didn't play about my time with him. My son's mother started giving me all kinds of excuses for why he couldn't come; he was sick, etc. I started to get gassed up (full of myself), making stupid threats because I was operating on my emotions. I finally got her to bring my son to a Walgreens parking lot. When we met, I was still cooling off, so I just grabbed him and dipped home. I didn't see all the abuse written on his body like a story from a book.

At the time, my son was only two years old, but he was very well spoken. I asked him why he had marks on him and he replied, "Timmy put me in a cold bath and put a garbage can over my head for hitting my little brother." My son had bruises on his body from a grown man?! I instantly became the maddest I have ever been in my life. I felt like those cartoon characters whose heads blow out fire from the top to express the anger they feel.

I had two choices, but I was so mad I thought I only had one. Remember, I spent most of my young life in the streets where everyone's mindset is a fixed one, and the belief is that only violence solves problems. I went to my room, put my shoes on and went to walk out the door when my mama said something that changed my life forever. "You can either be the man they expect you to, or you can be the man they don't expect you to; it's up to you!" I stopped right where I was and looked her in the eye, and when I did, what she said hit me like a ton of bricks. I instantly felt a power that I still to this day can't explain.

See our emotions are unavoidable. We don't have control over them, but we do have control over what we do with that energy. Self-control is an advantage we are given in life when it comes to emotions; where your focus goes your energy flows. Instead of taking that negative energy and using it to hurt someone, I used it to self-appoint myself as my lawyer and win custody of my son. I kept what my mama said, and the principle I have to be the best father I can because I didn't have mine, at the forefront of my mind. I faced all types of adversity that tested my character, and since that was a principle I valued, it helped me stay disciplined and kept my emotions in check. It will take time to create discipline behind all the things you value in life, but what helped me the most was having a "why" behind them. Emotions are temporary, but principles last a lifetime.

When I realized I couldn't base decisions on solely on emotion, I committed to creating principles that helped me navigate life and make good choices no matter how I felt. Sometimes your beliefs may change because of life experiences and maturity, but most people have principles they aren't even aware they have. These beliefs influence our decision making and actions. Here are a few examples of principles you may want to consider applying in your life.

9 PRINCIPLES OF LIFE

No Strain, No Gain

If you don't put in enough effort or work hard, you improve NOTHING. When you go through difficult times you learn more than you think; trust it's part of the process.

Avoid Negativity at All Cost

The society we live in has enough negativity from our homes to the media, which controls most of what we see and hear. You are going to have to deal with enough in life. Why deal with something you don't have to? Avoid the avoidable!

Give More Than You Take

Instead of always focusing on what you want from the world, start thinking about what you can offer. When you concentrate on making more deposits than withdrawals, you will always have something in the bank when you need it.

Time is More Valuable Than Money

Out of all the resources in the world, time is the most precious resource you have. You can lose money and still make it, but you can't turn back the hands of time.

Create Your Path

We look at others and view them as examples. Learning from others is one of the best things that I've done. Being humble is a good thing. You're not all those people though; you are YOU. Get off the beaten path and create your own! You can learn a lot from others, but you must bring your individuality and CREATE!

Do Whatever Life Expects of You

Instead of wishing that things were different, accept the circumstances of your life. No matter how bad it is, things are what they are. Regardless of where you are in life, God, the universe, invisible forces, etc., have you there for a reason.

People's Opinions of You Are Not Who You Are

You are the only person who decides who you are. Everyone seems to have a bright idea about how other people should lead their lives, but none about his or her own.

You're Going to Fail at Things

The only way to succeed is to fail; you must figure out what doesn't work to know what does. Failure is giving up and abandoning. Success is making mistakes, learning valuable lessons from those mistakes, and continuing with the process.

Accept Yourself Exactly as You Are, But Never Stop Trying to Learn and Grow

You must accept who you are, but that's not enough. You must also continue to add value to yourself, by learning and putting yourself in environments that will further develop you.

Efforts and courage are not enough without purpose and direction.

—Steve Maraboli.

08 GRIND FOR A REASON, NOT A SEASON

The grind is a continuous process of resistance done for a certain amount of time to create a result. The outcome can be negative or positive, draining or gaining, and everything we do in life that takes effort comes from the grind. When an individual pushes his/herself to attain a goal, they are grinding. The words "grind" and "grinding" in this context are more commonly used in urban culture and sports. The grinding is an unexciting, repetitive, sometimes difficult task done over an extended period. The grind is not about the excitement of the process or how you look completing the process

You grind hard towards something you want, need, or desire. All the blood, sweat, tears, lessons, wins, and dedication creates a residue I call the "grind residue" (a small amount of something that remains after the central part has gone or been taken or used.) It's the effect that is left from the work you consistently put in. Regardless of what you choose to obtain with your grind, negative or positive, there will be residue. You can choose to use the residue as momentum for your grind, or you can choose to use it as a brake to stop it. The residue is created by all the achievements, losses, experiences, growth, knowledge, uncertainty, and challenges you go through during the process. When you realize that the residue is a product of the grind, you will understand why the process is the most critical part.

Most people become motivated when they see positive results that are building toward the desired outcome. But what happens when it doesn't work out, and you have a bunch of unwanted residues? The residue can be turned into a lesson. You have a choice. If you are grinding for a reason and not a season, there will be a reason attached to your desire to succeed; if not, your passion will soon fade, just like the seasons. When you grind for a season, your desire fades, and your ambition does as well; your energy is wasted over a short period trying to obtain a quick reward. Instead, grind for a reason, and spend your energy getting long-term gain and success over an extended period.

Anything that comes fast and easy doesn't last long. Anything that takes time will be fruitful and well worth it. This principle of reaping huge rewards from a series of small, thoughtful choices that create success, or suffering from small, inconsiderate decisions that create misfortune, is a pillar to success. What's most interesting about this process to me is that, even when the results are massive, the steps, at the moment, don't feel significant. When I learned how to grind for a reason and not a season it started to make sense. Our current reality is an outcome of the little disciplines and decisions we do daily. That eventually adds up to your final grades, quality of life, overall health, income, relationships, and so much more.

When you repeat something over and over, it becomes a habit. Habits are things we do without putting much thought into it; a behavior pattern regularly followed until it has become almost instinctive. We all have habits and operate based on what they are. If you have a habit of being lazy, you will be lazy without trying to be, and if you have a habit of being driven, you will be that way without having to be pushed. It's complicated but straightforward because patterns make up the fabric of who we are. So, when you have lousy habits, they will affect your success negatively, and if you have good habits, they will help create your success. Most successful people have routines and daily disciplines that are habits formed o time.

YOU —> CHOICE + BEHAVIOR + HABIT + COMPOUNDED = GOALS

   (decision)   (action)   (repeated action)   (time)

Section 2
REAPING AND SOWING

"What's simple to do is also simple not to do."

Bottom line is you reap what you sow! You eventually have to face up to the consequences of your actions. These small changes offer little or no immediate result, no significant win, no apparent I-told-you-so payoff. So why bother? The magic is not in the complexity of the task; the magic is in the doing of simple things repeatedly and long enough to ignite the miracle that comes from following the process.

You know that old saying "what goes around, comes around?" It's a fair warning to us. Everything that we do has repercussions, be them good or bad, and it comes back to us one way or another. Don't ever be fooled into thinking that your actions don't have consequences. You reap what you sow.

As with the butterfly, adversity is necessary to build character in people.

—Joseph B. Wirthlin

09 ADVERSITY BREEDS EXCELLENCE

What do you do when life slaps you upside your head? Do you take it out on the world around you? Do you throw a fit like a child who cannot have his/her way? Are you one who remains calm only if life goes along with your plan? If so, I don't know what else to tell you other than the truth, which is that you're going to have to learn how to suck it up! Adversity is difficulties, misfortune, problems, distress, and challenge. Most people think it is all bad, but they don't know that it can build character. You cannot build solid muscle for strength without eating protein and get exercising (say, for instance, lifting weights). No, to be effective, you have to go outside your comfort zone. It's a process, and you have to learn to endure the hardest parts of life first, to have the strength to handle what life has in store for you next. Adversity is for your life what protein is for your body.

You need to be challenged to grow. As you successfully overcome challenges, you build resilience, which creates a muscle that helps your ability to face and overcome other challenges.

I know we understand the adverse effects that difficulty has on us, but I want to focus on challenging you to look at it with a different perspective. Everyone has had some form of adversity in their life or will at some point; especially those traveling the road success. Look at the Bible for example. Now, I'm not trying to get all religious, but all the stories told have something in common. Do you know what that commonality is? I'll wait.... Adversity, right? Yes! The Bible isn't the only place you can find stories that began with difficulty and ended with success; it's also in every history book and a part of any process that produces a worthwhile reward.

Even in nature, we see examples of the positive effects adversity can have. For example, coal is transformed into diamonds only as a result of heat and pressure. Protect a piece of coal from "hardship," and it will remain unimproved. The same will happen to you if you don't experience challenges in life. You have to embrace the process of becoming a diamond and endure the pressure and heat that comes with it; otherwise, you remain a piece of coal, never to become what you were truly meant to be.

From the examples, it should be clear how adversity makes people stronger in every way. Since you can't avoid adversity, you may as well learn to appreciate its benefits. When you recognize the significant role adversity plays in your success, your mental attitude becomes more positive, and your discomfort isn't as intense when faced with adversity. The next time you encounter a struggle, treat it as an opportunity instead of the end of the world. Doing this will empower you to use it as a stepping stone instead of feeling crushed by it. With each adversity you overcome, you will gain invaluable knowledge while growing stronger.

Individuals who run from adversity allow themselves to become worn down by it. As they do everything they can to avoid difficulty, they seem to attract more of it into their lives. How is this possible? I believe that whatever you give energy is what you give power. If this is the case, then fear causes you to focus your energy on what you don't want, which results in you giving it the power to manifest. Appreciate challenge rather than becoming discouraged by it. It takes constant awareness to avoid becoming stuck in the struggle. Remember, since adversity is an unavoidable part of life, as well as being essential for success, you may as well have a positive attitude about it.

Adversity develops good character, which is an essential quality in a person. Whether it be in our professional, educational, or personal lives, it is important to associate with people of good character. But what is character exactly? Character is the mental and moral qualities an individual has. A person with good mental and moral character chooses on their own to do the right thing, regardless of the situation. Character has to be developed; I wouldn't find out exactly how until I was 18 and already going through a trial for my criminal cases and later my son's custody battle.

I knew that I didn't have to go to prison. I could have taken a deal or snitched, but I didn't see it as an option. It wasn't the right thing to do. Even when I fought for custody of my son, I didn't have to do that; I could have just left things the way they were. I didn't see that as an option either, however. I hadn't always exercised good character in the past, but if I was going to change my life, that needed to change with it. So, during those experiences, I decided to start doing what was right. No one told me to or put a gun to my head; I started doing it of my own will. Through all of my experiences, I found that character is developed over time as you go through the ups and downs of life, and by working towards something positive.

Today I strive to live the definition of good character, but I've had my share of adversity to help build it. My previous struggles had left me feeling lost, hopeless, and worst of all mad at the world. That attitude led me to some questionable life decisions. I quit school and traded any chance of self-improvement for the instant gratification that came from selling drugs and hustling. After a while, I realized that I was making money, but I was also making my problems worse. My lack of good character positioned me for prison, but my development of it has now positioned me for greatness.

You know that saying, "it's always darkest before the dawn?" It's true. Just when I was feeling defeated, almost ready to give up and settle for my losses in life, things started to turn around for me. Nothing significant at first, small wins, but the improvement in my life became noticeable once my attitude started to improve. The more time went by, the more I began to see my past for what it was, the past.

Adversity breeds good character, this I believe to be true. Through my personal experiences, I found that hardship is a life lesson, not some form of punishment delivered by karma. I accepted that I couldn't change the unfortunate events in my life, but I could look at them differently. Life is all about perspective, and I had to endure the bad to appreciate the good in it.

I remember reading some book or watching some video talking about how we make choices and how the results of those decisions aren't always good, even when we have great intentions. Even still, we should always try and make the best choice. I thought about this for awhile; I weighed my pros and cons. When I started thinking about my future, I decided that if I struggled, hit adversity, or found myself lost, it would be with good intention and unselfishly based. I had been locked away from my family and friends when they needed me the most due to selfish, bad intentions; I wasn't going to allow it to happen again.

> *"The ultimate measure of a man is not where he stands in moments of comfort and convenience, but where he stands at times of challenge and controversy."*
>
> **Martin Luther King Jr.**

As with the butterfly, adversity is necessary to build character in people.

—Joseph B. Wirthlin

10 THE I 'AM WORTHY' PHILOSOPHY

This chapter is personal and has a lot of meaning to why I wrote this book. I honestly believe that no matter what you have been through, you have a value. Each one of us in this world has a purpose; it doesn't matter how big or small. What is important is that you have unlimited potential to accomplish this at the highest level imaginable. We have a role in this world, and sometimes we forget this. It's not any less or more important than the rest of the roles because every role has an integral part in creating the fabric which built this country and all the others.

Now I'm not saying that it's promised to you, but if you are willing to work hard for it, you will accomplish many things in life. If we received the benefits of our gifts up front, there would be no point in the process. It's the journey, experiences, and how we get there that makes them such rewards.

Embrace it while you chase it is saying while you are on this journey you must truly embrace everything. The process in between, the practice, times you want to give up, and the moments all the hard work pays off. It's what will make you great! Not just achieving your goals and dreams but what you went through to get it and that's what makes it all worth it.

I started this brand "I AM WORTHY" in 2016, and it has turned into a movement. I started a business empowering young people, and it spread!!! Now I'm living in my purpose, which is why I am writing a book on the principles that helped me break the stigmas, stereotypes, and cycles in my life that were holding me back from reaching my potential. These principles are the necessary things I needed to add value to who I am. This information isn't everything, and there is an exception to every rule or principle, but it has created a foundation for me to transform my life from selling dope to selling hope and turning negatives into positives.

I AM WORTHY is not just a brand; it's a way of living and an affirmation. You're declaring that you have self-worth and deserve whatever you want if you are willing to fight, sacrifice, and believe that you're deserving of it. As an affirmation, it gives you power. "Worthy" is associated with empowerment, and "I AM" are two of the most influential words you can say to yourself. There is nothing more important than for you to know your self-worth. What you think of yourself, whether your capable or incapable, is stronger than you can imagine. Just because you aren't doing or can't do something at first, doesn't mean you're not worth anything. That is where the hard work, sacrifice, and belief comes in.

I only have a GED while writing this book and building my business, but everyone I work around has a college education. I didn't let that determine my worth. My passion pushed me to self-educate myself, go out and get experience, and develop the advantageous life experiences I already have. So, the value comes from bringing what you have to the table and building on top of that. We all have unlimited potential; the problem is we don't realize it.

You've allowed everyone else to determine your value, but I'm here to tell you that that's your job. It's for you to declare and activate your worth.

Any idea or opportunity you have is yours, and it's on you to make it happen. I'm just here to remind you of something straightforward; you are WORTHY of it! It may take some time and work to figure that out, but you are. I have been locked up as both a juvenile and an adult. I have sold drugs and robbed people and plenty other wrong things. The one thing I always had that I didn't utilize well though was a choice.

When I decided to make better decisions, everything started to change. I went from being fatherless to a full custody father. From prison inmate to Founder/CEO of my own company. I still live on my terms and didn't have to change much except my mindset and the views I held about myself and the world. As Kendall Ficklin told me once "it's the same hustle, different product or service." I have the same hustle and the same passion I've always had, just a different approach to how I use it.

I figured out how to make myself an asset, but it took time. The two most important things I can say I did was make sure I was positive, and that I had a purpose behind me. I'm not here to tell you what to do, but I hope I helped you see that you can make life worthwhile just as I did. You can do and be whatever and whoever you want, but you must be the one to discover your purpose, work hard to fulfill it, and embrace the adversity that comes while you're chasing it. No matter your past or how difficult the journey becomes, remain loyal to the process and affirm to yourself every day "I AM WORTHY."

Self-worth comes from one thing, thinking that you are WORTHY!

Wayne Dyer

> *A champion is afraid of losing.*
> *Everyone else is afraid*
> *of winning.*
>
> *—Billie Jean King*

11 WHY YOU AREN'T WINNING (BONUS CHAPTER)

I started winning because I got tired! I got tired of not having, not being, and tired of settling for less. I was tired of looking at people who were no more capable than I, get what I wanted, strive for things I wanted to strive for and create the kind of life for themselves that I also wanted to have. I had a problem with complaining about "losing" but not being fed up enough to do something about it. So, I began to concentrate on "winning," and that's when everything changed. The word "winning" means to gain or relates to victory in a contest or competition. You compete with yourself and whatever holds you back from your endeavors. It is a contest that you and the odds against you both enter, but your skills, willpower, and overall beliefs determine who wins. When you overcome your obstacles and struggles, you deserve to shine!

There is a basic motivation to improve yourself that either develops out of inspiration to become better than you already are or out of desperation because something unpleasant is challenging you to grow. For example, I went to jail in 2008 when my son was born. I was on the path to becoming the same type of man my father was to me "a sucka." No disrespect, but I think as men we have both an obligation and a right to provide for and be a part of our children's lives regardless of what it costs us because they need us. I'm not saying the system is always fair or anything like that. What I'm saying is that even when it's not, we should still try to be around through the drama and hard times so our children can have the support they need to develop properly.

I wasn't going to let anyone get in the way of me being in my son's life, even though literally all odds were against me. I didn't know if I would win custody, but I knew I wasn't going to be able to sleep knowing I didn't try to do what I could. I know I'm not a "sucka," do you? The ball is in your court. Whatever you are up against, you can either overcome the odds or be defeated by not trying at all. Many individuals think that because you don't obtain the goal, you fail. No, the failure is when you don't try or just give up.

My issue had nothing to do with jealousy or envy and everything to do with my self-worth. I thought people were superhuman or possessed a magical power that I didn't have. I never placed the responsibility on myself, the only person who could change my circumstances. I had to realize that "I AM WORTHY" of anything I choose to pursue if I'm willing to work for it. No one determines your worth except you, and no one knows your potential except you.

The definition of "winning" in this chapter isn't just making money, having materialistic items, etc. Winning is making life work for you on your terms no matter what. This is something that goes much deeper than it sounds, but that can work for anyone. There are examples of people who have had a lot worse situations compared to yours but still made "winning" work for them.

When I see people born without limbs like Nick Vujicic or Richie Park, I find it hard to complain and not take responsibility for my own life. We can talk about race, sex, and other factors, but not having limbs is extreme. Nick Vujicic was born without arms and legs and has managed to become one of the top motivational speakers in the world. He is also an author and married with kids. Please google him and read his story.

Richie Parker was born with no arms and is an engineer for Hendrick Motorsports, a NASCAR Company. Every task these men perform takes some level of intelligence, ambition, and willpower. Even with the odds they had against them, they found a way to make life work for them. Please google Richie as well.

I want to make sure I'm honest and transparent with what I'm saying, even if it makes you feel uncomfortable. When you are placed in difficult situations, it provides you with a challenge needed to grow and become a better person. I had to hear the truth from many different places, and with that information, I had to make adjustments to my life. The central principle of this process is to learn to take ownership of every area of your life. One of the toughest things to do is to listen to what you aren't doing right and how you could be better, but it will stop growth and keep you from getting to another level if you don't understand how significant it is to develop through feedback.

We can learn from every situation we go through if we allow ourselves to keep an open mind, continually evaluate who we are, and put consistent effort in developing who we are.

1. Keeping an open mind will allow you to notice things you may not have in the past because of your own bias. We all have biases, but when we have an open mind, we don't allow those biases to affect our perspective; which is essential because we don't know everything and can always learn.

2. Being able to assess who you are continually is like the captain of a ship sailing in an ocean but referring back to a compass every now and again to figure out which way to go or make sure they are on the right path. You can't expect to grow or become anything without assessing yourself. If you evaluate your performance, production, learning, application, development, and many other things, you will develop and get better. Focusing on turning talent into skill, average into phenomenal, and nothing into something forces you to assess yourself in many ways.

3. Personal Development is the conscious pursuit of personal growth by expanding self-awareness and knowledge and

improving individual skills. It is a significant ingredient for success. If you aren't willing to develop, then you won't make it very far. The goal is to create growth and enhancement in all aspects; mentally, physically, and spiritually.

How to Start Personal Development

1. **Engage in honest self-reflection and create a sense of awareness.**

   I think it takes some time and honesty to become self-aware, but if you reflect daily, it will help. It's important to do this so you can evaluate yourself and become better. You will be doing this for life, especially if you want to develop personally.

2. **Create Goals and Vision**

   Without a clear idea of what you want and how that looks, it's going to be hard to navigate where you're going or how to get there. When you have a vision, it's easier to create goals, and when you have goals, you can develop in areas needed to accomplish them.

3. **Consume Information and Content**

   "You are what you eat" is very similar to "you are what you consume." Meaning the information, you obtain from videos, podcast, etc., develops you into the person you are. `If you're not consuming information that is going to help you accomplish your goals, why are you taking it in? I'm not saying don't entertain yourself, but stop confusing entertainment with development.

4. **Push yourself past your limits**

    You will not develop in your comfort zone. People have to push themselves to build real skill. It takes going past what you think your limit is and tapping deep into your potential. You have to stop letting people, T.V., and other things place boundaries on your abilities. Once you start to stretch yourself, you will be amazed at how flexible you are.

5. **5. Experience is the best teacher**

    Most people learn more by doing something than by reading about it. There is no substitute for experience, and there is no faster way to learn than to do! We remember the lessons we learned by doing for a long time and always remember not to repeat mistakes. On the other hand, if we learn from our friends and families, we forget those things pretty fast, as we didn't go through the process ourselves. We often overlook their tips and advice from what they learned. But, when we go through the obstacles and hurdles ourselves, we experience the whole process. These hands-on experiences help us to remember our journey and keep us prepared for a long time.

6. **6. If you don't love it, don't do it**

    There are going to be plenty of times when you have to do things you don't want to do; it may be in your best interest, be attached to something that you will benefit from, or be a necessary part of a process in life you have to go through. To push through and do them anyway, you need to attach meaning to them. This will help you stay committed. There will be points in life when you feel as though you do not have very much control over doing what you love, but as long as you keep working towards it, you will eventually get to the place you want to at.

At some point in your life, you have to take responsibility for you. Stop letting your environment, current circumstances, and disadvantages determine your value and self-worth. You have to dig deep inside of who you are and strive to bring that to light, no matter how dark it may be at that moment. I am speaking to the gang members, people living in poverty, the mentally ill, the neglected and abused; the list goes on and on. If you don't fit in the box society has built for you then I'm challenging you to break the stigmas, stereotypes, and cycles.

Winners can't have conversations with losers because they don't speak the same language.

Section 1
MUTUAL VALUE RULE

I have a principle that I live by; unfortunately, I didn't always live by it in my past. When you find the value in having this rule or principle as a part of your life, you will experience less stress, drama, toxic relationships, etc. Any "ship" that you have in life make it mandatory that this principle applies. When I say "ship," I mean relationship, membership, partnership, companionship, friendship; any "ship." Mutual value means exchanging value between two interested parties. Those parties would be you and whatever "ship" you enter into. If you give value but don't receive value in return, you need to "abandon 'ship!'"

I believe the world works better when you have people around you who are providing as much value as they are receiving. When you have a mutual exchange, there is a deeper meaning to the "ship," and it can take you places you never imagined. If there is no value, think of it as dragging an anchor through the ocean as you are trying to sail. Sooner or later it's going to cause complications in your journey.

The mutual value rule has a unique process; the value isn't always viewed as equal, but the only person who determines that is you. Loyalty could be priceless to a millionaire, so he does everything he can for anyone who is loyal to him, so individuals are loyal to the millionaire in exchange for needed resources the millionaire offers.

Famous people do this all of the time for friends, family, business partners, etc. The values may not seem equal, but there is an old saying that "one man's trash is another man's treasure." What you might consider invaluable might be gold to another person.

When you move through life, remember this saying because you don't always need money to be in a circle with millionaires; sometimes you just need to provide value in a way that they don't. So think about using this principle in more areas of your life too. I have started to use this principle in any way possible. It's an easy way to get value for your value and not allow others to just take from you without providing anything.

My whole college experience has been based on the Mutual Value Rule. I thought about how much that degree would separate me from my peers in my field and how many opportunities would come from it. I knew I could add value to my program of study and school too. I have already done a keynote presentation there to seniors who are about to graduate. I told my story and how I am embracing education with my passion and purpose attached. I will hire and give internships to students going through the program as well. It has been almost a year since I enrolled and I have already received many opportunities from being a student and pursuing an education in the field I have a passion for and own a business in; that to me is one of the best values. Now when I graduate and continue my journey, individuals will enroll because I spoke about and wore that school on my back with pride.

People are out here wasting their time and complaining about things they allow and accept in there lives. YOU choose to be with someone, deal with something, or involve yourself in a situation. Keeping this principle in your mind will help you navigate through situations and "ships" in a way that doesn't require conflict, violence, or wasting your time; the one thing we can't get back. It's important to place value on choosing who we give the privilege of sharing our value with. It doesn't matter who, what, or where. If we don't place value on who gets ours then how precious is it?

So please keep this principle with you in life. You will benefit tremendously in many ways, from avoiding unwanted drama and energy-sucking leeches who act like friends, to preventing the investment of time into worthless "ships" and commitments.

Section 2
SMALL WINS

In the book, The Power of Habits, Charles Duhigg uses the term "small wins" to describe the small behavior changes that can shift a chain reaction of changes. Creating small wins in your life through practice and repetition will eventually become a habit.

A small win is exactly what it sounds like, a small victory in your day or life. As humans, we are built to naturally see the problems and easily punish ourselves for bad behavior. Our mindsets can bring us down when we feel we've failed and this usually results in giving up on dreams and goals. Instead of looking at your big goal and getting frustrated at how much work there is to start off with, the key to being successful is realizing that those goals aren't going to be accomplished overnight and adapting small wins. Break your big and goals down into small actions that you can do that will over time, achieve the big goal. Another way to adapt small wins is to change your mindset, behavior, or habits. "The Power of Habits" talks a lot about this. While doing research and learning about habits, something hit me. One of the hardest things for a human to do is be consistent, especially when trying to create habits, because as easy as it is to say "quit smoking," it's much harder to break the habit and develop a new one through consistency.

I use small wins in a lot of my youth sessions, and I talk about how important it is to assess yourself. Sometimes we go through life only focused on the big things and don't see how much of a deal it is to pay attention to the small ones too. People complain and become negative because that's what they pay attention to or look for. They never pay attention to the little positive things that happen such as being alive, being able to walk and talk, etc. Those small, positive things outweigh the negative ones. The problem is society pushes you to think that everything needs to happen now or overnight, but that's not realistic at all. So we take advantage of small, simple things or believe that they don't matter; which is not true. Without those small, simple actions there would be no significant results. Focusing on celebrating the small wins will help you develop habits for more significant wins.

Examples of small wins can be:

- Getting a job (putting you in a position to obtain more and better opportunities)
- Finding a new circle of friends (getting out of bad environments and unhealthy relationships)
- Hitting 10 jump shots in a row (developing a skill)
- Making your bed when you get out of it (creating habits)
- Raising your grades
- Replacing negative thoughts with positive ones daily
- Losing a pound

ABOUT THE AUTHOR

As a young man, adolescence was hard to navigate. My dad, though actively willing to cheat, lie, and steal (he took anything from social security numbers to cars) to get high, was not actively ready to be a father. He wasn't in my life then, and he still isn't today.

My mother was moving forward away from her past life, and working towards a career in the aerospace industry. She had her ups and downs but managed to keep me together and always made sure she provided and didn't have to depend on a man for her survival. My mother remarried when I was about two years old, and I grew up in a blue-collar household, as both she and my stepfather were laborers at Boeing Company; they made a living building airplane parts.

I grew up playing sports, and although my parents did the best they could, I didn't have a support system due to the shifts they worked; having them at games was a miracle I looked forward to. I acted out everywhere to get the attention I wasn't receiving at home and grew up too fast running in the streets. At 17 I moved out to an area known as Lakewood and decided to try to make it on my own living at a friend's house. I was always trying to manipulate people and finesse my way into anything I could. I was just like my father, even though I had never met the man or even knew what he looked like.

Without having positive influences like mentors or older brothers in my life, I quickly turned to the wrong people for guidance and went down the wrong life path. I started smoking weed and selling drugs. I didn't have to sell drugs; my family wasn't starving or anything like that, I just wanted my own money. I would watch how hard my mama worked and saw how much she did for our family; I didn't want to bother her and sometimes she just didn't have it. They taught me the value of hard-work ethics, but the truth is I chose to make money selling drugs because I didn't like authority or working for anyone, so I didn't buy into the "get a job" thing.

Running the streets and selling drugs landed me in court four years later. I was looking at ten years for two delivery charges and two-gun charges. I made it through this and other adversities in my life using the principles in this book. Now I'm a single, full custody father and CEO/Founder of IAMWorthy & Associates LLC, a mentoring and youth development direct service business, out to empower young people by teaching them leadership and life skills.

The information in this book took me years to learn, and I want to share it with you because I believe that if I had been informed, I would have looked at and approached life differently in the beginning.

Even if I hadn't, I would still be aware of what's happening now and how it's affecting me; from serving time in prison to becoming a full custody father. Throughout my 28 years of life, I have seen and done a lot of things; much of which could have been avoided had I had the insight I have now.

So when I speak and write, it's on things I have been through and with messages that I hope you can relate to. These principles are attached to experiences in my life. The information connects with things I have learned from books, people, personal experience, and other resources I used to develop myself and transform my life.

Through time, they have become high values I believe in. They help me navigate through life, like a moral compass. You might not need certain principles from this book in your life, but I do want you to take what you can apply from it and find your own principles to live by.

Shaun Worthy

www.ingramcontent.com/pod-product-compliance
Lightning Source LLC
Chambersburg PA
CBHW072036160426
43198CB00029B/2289